5024

To Pete

Happy Christmas   1986

GROWING
UNDER GLASS

(ILLUSTRATED)

by

GEORGE H. COPLEY

*National Diploma in Horticulture ; Joint Organizer Lancashire
County Garden Produce and Small Livestock Committee ;
Horticultural Consultant ; Member of Gardeners'
Brains Trusts*

Author of

PESTS AND DISEASES OF VEGETABLES
FRUIT GROWING
TOMATO GROWING FOR THE AMATEUR
MANURING FOOD CROPS
MUSHROOMS AND OTHER CROPS
HOW TO MANAGE AN ALLOTMENT
WILD FLOWERS AND WEEDS
ETC.

A
JOHN CROWTHER
PUBLICATION
1945

The typography and binding
of this book conform to the
authorized economy standard

Made and Printed in Great Britain by
BOBBY & CO. LTD., Printers, MARGATE, for
JOHN CROWTHER LTD., BOGNOR REGIS and
14, HENRIETTA PLACE, LONDON, W.1, ENGLAND

AGENTS : NEW YORK . TORONTO . MELBOURNE

PRELUDE

❧

THERE is no more fascinating pursuit than that of growing food crops under glass. The gardener feels a greater confidence than he does with outdoor crops, because the conditions are protected. It matters not whether there is rain, hail, snow, frost or wind out of doors, his treasures are safe. And in many cases very early, out-of-season yields can be secured. They appeal, for every man and woman likes something unusual. Moreover, out-of-season crops are, in the present emergency, helpful in the national interest. That emergency may not last long so far as the clash of arms is concerned, but it will on the food front. Many years must elapse before the international situation is normal.

Under-glass gardening requires a special technique. I have in this book endeavoured, in simple language, to set forth that technique. All the suggestions are born of practical experience, a teacher with unquestionable credentials.

George H. Copley.

1944.

INDEX

❧

GROWING UNDER GLASS

Chapter I

GREENHOUSES AND FRAMES

IF British gardening were confined to the cultivation of plants that are hardy in conditions similar to those which prevail in the country, the need for glass structures, by which I mean greenhouses, frames and cloches, would be nothing like as extensive as it is to-day. Such a type of horticulture would, however, be very limited in its scope. It would not be as interesting and profitable as it is now. We grow plants from all parts of the world, and as many of these need protection, it is essential to grow them under a covering of glass, which may be heated or unheated, according to the requirements of the kind. Moreover, some of the hardy subjects which we grow out of doors in Summer are cultivated under glass in Winter for the purpose of securing out-of-season crops.

Examples that come readily to mind are lettuce, French beans, peas, radishes, potatoes, globe beet, and so on. The scope is tremendous, and I cannot imagine that any follower of man's first calling, whether he be professional or amateur, is going to be happy very long unless he includes in his operations one or more forms of under-glass gardening. I am going to assume, in writing this book, that my readers have little or no knowledge of the subject, and that I am teaching them from the very beginning. I feel that to be essential, because as I go about on my various occasions connected with the food production campaign, I find that results would be better if foundation principles were grasped.

THE GREENHOUSE

There are three main types of greenhouse—span-roof, three-quarters span, and lean-to. Of this trio the first-named is undoubtedly the best, because it receives the most light which, of course, is the great life-giving factor. Often it is essential to shade a span-roof greenhouse at certain periods of the year, but conditions are under complete control. They can be shaded or unshaded, according to the need.

It follows, therefore, that since the value of a span-roof greenhouse derives from the light it receives, the structure should be in a sunny position. Unless there is some over-riding objection, it is an advantage if the greenhouse runs north and south. In this aspect the sun rises on the east side, at noon his rays are evenly distributed, in the afternoon the west side of the house derives the major benefit. Thus, taking the day as a whole, no part of the house receives favoured treatment. I would not, however, suggest that plants will not succeed in a green-house built in any other light aspect. They certainly will, but those who are constructing will naturally desire to follow the highest principles.

A three-quarters span greenhouse is a house which has glass at both ends, on one side, and part of the way down the other. The remainder of the latter is a brick wall or a fence. Opaque material of this kind, of course, excludes light, but the plants in the house receive sufficient of this vital factor for healthy growth if the structure runs east and west. That is to say, if the bulk of the glass faces south.

A lean-to house is built alongside a wall or fence. It is, in fact, half a complete span, but here again, if the house runs east and west, and the glass side faces south, abundant light enters. It will be necessary to turn the plants round occasionally, to keep them shapely and erect, for they will inevitably draw to the south.

6

CONSTRUCTIONAL DETAILS

There are many points to watch in the building of a greenhouse. Not the least important of these is the angle or slope of the roof. If the house is to be used for intensive forcing, such as the growing of early fruit, the roof should have an angle of forty-four degrees. That is to say, it should rise eleven inches per foot. For general purposes, that is, for the cultivation of the big range of plants in which most gardeners are interested, the angle should be twenty-six degrees, or a rise of six inches per foot.

The height of the greenhouse is primarily a matter for each gardener to decide. For average requirements ten feet is suitable. Such a house should be twelve to fifteen feet wide, and have a two feet wide path down the centre. The height to the eaves should be six feet, and it is always an advantage if the greenhouse rests on a three feet brick foundation. Brick is much warmer than wood, and is much more durable.

As greenhouses, owing to the amount of water used in them, are more subject to deterioration than average buildings, it is imperative to use well seasoned deal or red cedar. The latter type of wood has advanced greatly in favour during recent years. I emphasize this matter because I have often seen amateurs building greenhouses out of very unsuitable spare wood, which before very long would either warp badly, or begin to decay. When one is expending money on a structure of this kind, it is obviously more economic to use the right type of material, even though it costs a little more. It is cheaper in the end.

HEATING AND VENTILATION

Greenhouses can be heated by coke or coal-fed boilers, fume-proof oil stoves, or by electricity. From the horticultural standpoint these three methods are sound. As they stand at present, for reasons which I will indicate later, I prefer the coke or coal-fed boiler and hot water pipes. For houses up to ten feet in length, one row of four inch piping is essential, a flow and a return. A more even heat is generated if the flow runs along one side of the house, and the return comes down the other to the boiler.

For larger houses I favour two rows of four inch piping—two flows and two returns. It will not be necessary on many occasions to drive the boiler to its full capacity, and that is a great advantage. A heating apparatus that is well master of its work is worry-free. When continual driving is essential, there is no peace for the stoker. Four inch pipes are better than two inch pipes because it is not necessary to heat them so much in order to maintain the temperature. A bigger volume of water is casting its kindly influence into the house, and is not adversely affecting the growing atmosphere as much as an overheated pipe does. That is the reason why conditions are more congenial to plant life in a greenhouse warmed by a coke or coal-fed boiler than they are in a house warmed by any other known method.

Nevertheless, the fume-proof oil stoves are doing excellent work. If kept clean and well trimmed they do their job splendidly. The drier atmosphere they create can be overcome by more frequent damping down. It is desirable to watch very carefully, for though this type of apparatus is built to be fume-proof, it is made and tended by human hands, which can err. Should at any time an oily smell emanate from the apparatus, correct the fault forthwith, for the fumes do great harm in a short time.

I have no doubt that the future holds great possibilities for electrical heating. I visualize the time when all that we shall need to do will be to turn on a switch, and the temperature of our greenhouses will be thermostatically controlled at the desired level. This can now be done, and from the purely electrical, technical standpoint, the apparatus is most efficient, but the heat is what gardeners call a dry heat, in which plant life is not particularly happy. I agree that atmospheric humidity can be created by the use of moisture, but this is making up a defect which will, I hope, in course of time be remedied by the makers themselves.

Moreover, the cost of electrical heating is at the moment rather heavy. It is generally agreed by gardeners that when electricity for heating greenhouses can be sold at one farthing per unit, it will be as economic as other forms of heating, but not before.

Provision must be made for ventilating the house, and where possible, ventilators should be fixed on both sides of a span and a three-quarters span, so that air can be admitted on the leeward side. In small houses roof ventilators are adequate. In addition, side ventilators should be installed in the larger type of house, and if these are controlled by levers, the labour of airing is greatly reduced.

GLASS AND NAILS

For greenhouses twenty-four ounce transparent glass is the best. It is, if properly puttied in, strong enough to resist gales, and is not easily broken by simple accidents. If the bottom of each pane of glass describes a curve, instead of being cut straight across, rain-water will be carried from the guts to the centre of each length of panes, and from them will run into the spouting. This arrangement greatly reduces the risk of decaying wood. An appropriate size of pane is twelve inches wide by ten inches long. Anything narrower than this increases the quantity of wood required, and the number of shadows that are thrown on to the plants beneath.

Use the minimum quantity of nails, as water follows the nail track, and shortens the life of the wood. Tenon and morticed joints are equally as effective, and are never the cause of deterioration.

9

STAGES

Unless the greenhouse is used entirely for the cultivation of plants or crops in permanent borders, a stage should be fixed on each side of the path as near to the roof of the house as is permissible after allowing head room for the plants. It is helpful if the stage is portable. In a small greenhouse, for example, a gardener may wish to

COLD FRAMES

Span frame to left of picture, half-span to right

grow tomatoes on the stage in Summer, and flower his chrysanthemums in the house in Autumn and Winter. He cannot do this if his stage is within three or four feet of the glass. He must take out that stage, and stand his chrysanthemums at ground level.

Those are the principal points that should be noted in the construction of a greenhouse.

THE COLD FRAME

Though not as ambitious as a greenhouse, a cold frame is a very valuable adjunct. There are two types—span-roof and half-span. The former, like the span-roof greenhouse, has two sides, with glass on each side. Its advantages are similar. There is an unbroken flow of light all the day to all parts of the frame. I would like to see more span-roof frames in use. At present they are seldom met with, except in large private gardens and commercial establishments. Many amateurs do not know about them at all.

The situation for a frame should be in full light, giving shade as and when necessary. A suitable height at the sides is twenty-four inches, a suitable ridge height thirty inches. The individual lights must not be too large, or they will be heavy to handle, and accidents may occur. Further, however many precautions are taken, there are times when the wind blows off a light, with consequences that can be imagined. The bigger the light, the greater the damage. I have tried many sizes, and find that the one five feet long by three feet wide is the most convenient.

It is in the interests of durability to build the sides of brick, and there should be a ventilator running from one end of the ridge to the other. This is lifted up by a small lever. Often one can ventilate by means of this ridge cap when the outdoor atmosphere is very cold, without admitting cold air directly on to the plants. There is no recognized limit to the number of lights, though I find it beneficial to have a wood division after every second light. This makes it possible to give the differential treatment which is out of the question under a long stretch of undivided lights.

THE HALF-SPAN FRAME

This is the type generally known and used, and a good type it is. The sides, back and front of the frame are of wood or brick. An appropriate back height is thirty inches, front height twenty-four inches, distance between back and front five feet, width of light three feet. Here again there is an advantage in not having too much space within one frame. There should be a division after every second light or, alternatively a number of two-light frames.

Where space permits, fix the half-span cold frames alongside the greenhouse. Not only does this arrangement economize material, but the greenhouse provides shelter, and by reflecting heat on to the frame, makes conditions more genial.

Chapter II

CROPS IN HEATED GREENHOUSES

DURING the past few years tomato growing has become the interest of almost everybody who possesses a heated greenhouse. The war has increased the interest, for tomatoes are a first line food. They are officially considered to be as good a substitute for citrus fruits as can be obtained in these times. The cultural problem is not difficult, but there are principles which must receive unfailing attention. If this were more generally realized, the yields would be far heavier than they are to-day. I now proceed to describe an all-success cultural programme.

SEED SOWING

May I stress the supreme necessity for obtaining a good strain of seed. The best treatment will not win a good crop from a poor stock. Reliable varieties are numerous. Kondine Red, Potentate and E.S.1 are examples. Seed may be sown from early November until the end of March. The best month for the amateur is February. Here is an ideal compost : Loam three parts, granulated peat (or leaf mould) and sand one part each. Pass the ingredients through a half-inch sieve, to ensure an even texture.

Use scrupulously clean seven-inch pots, seed-pans, or boxes, draining the pots and pans with a single layer of inverted crocks, covered with a two-inch layer of rough compost riddlings. Now fill up fairly firmly with compost to within half an inch of the top. Drain boxes with an inch layer of the riddlings only, afterwards filling up with compost. Space the seed an inch apart, cover it with silver or river sand, and place glass and brown paper over the vessels until the seedlings show.

TEMPERATURE AND CARE OF THE SEEDLINGS

An ideal temperature for the germination of the seed, and at all stages when fire heat is necessary, is sixty degrees Fahr. Of course, the thermometer will rise above this by sun heat. That does not matter, but it is important not to maintain a high artificial heat. Equally is it important not to allow the temperature to fall below sixty degrees Fahr. Artificial heat will not be needed all the season. Towards the end of May, depending on the weather, cease to use fire heat, but always be prepared to light the boiler later for a few days if we should pass through one of those cold, wet spells typical of average British Summers.

As soon as the seedlings show remove the covers, and give good light, though during the fragile early stages apply a little shade if the seedlings show embarrassment. Water carefully, using pure, aired water, and when the second normal leaf forms, transplant the seedlings at

two inches apart into other boxes, rejecting markedly
weak or abnormal specimens. The mixture advised for
seed sowing, with the addition of two ounces of National
Growmore or other complete fertilizer to the pailful,
is appropriate at this stage. Ventilate as freely as the
weather allows, but do avoid cold draughts.

TOMATO PROPAGATION.   PLANTS IN SIXTIES
(By kind permission of Dr. Bewley, Director Cheshunt Experimental and Research
Station)

POTTING THE PLANTS

Conceptions regarding tomato culture are continually
being modified by experiment and experience. Thus
it is not now considered necessary to pot the seedlings
first into thumb pots, then into the four and a half inch
size, and set some fruit on the bottom truss before moving
them to their permanent quarters. In fact, that method
may not always result in the best yield. A better practice
is to move the plants from the boxes into three-inch pots

before there is any sign of congestion. If they are watered very carefully after the final planting from these pots, growth will build up strongly, and there will be a bumper crop.

The compost suggested for transplanting into boxes is perfect for the potting. Use every care in handling the plants. If the stems are squeezed with the thumbs in the potting process, the check thus given may never be overcome. Pot fairly firmly, and after watering through a rosed can, stand the plants on a light shelf or stage. At this period tomatoes need more light than at any other stage of growth. The type of the plant is being decided, and the decision will only be right if there is uninterrupted light.

On bright days spray in the late afternoon with slightly aired water, but only on bright days. The object of the treatment is to keep growth supple without making it too succulent. After a fortnight to three weeks, knock out of their pots a typical plant or two, and note the progress that is being made. If white roots are working freely round the soil ball, prepare to plant in the final quarters. On no account must the tomatoes become pot-bound before they go there.

THE FINAL PLANTING

The final tomato compost is a most important factor. I am frequently called in to inspect unhealthy crops, and in nine cases out of ten the rooting medium is the cause of the trouble. May I say at once that tomatoes will not succeed in old potting soil, or any sort of mixture prepared at random ? The requirements of the crop as to texture and food supply must be met. Experience prompts me confidently to recommend the following mixture : Turf broken to walnut size four parts, well-rotted manure and sand one part each, with a five inch potful each of wood ashes, bone meal and soot to the barrowful. Turn over the ingredients three times, to get a good mixture, and before planting warm the latter in the greenhouse for three or four days.

Tomatoes may be planted in a nine inch wide, six inch high stage border, or separately in clean, well-drained, half-filled nine-inch pots, or boxes of comparable size. Top dressings must be given later, whichever method is adopted, but at the beginning it is inadvisable to surround the roots with too big a body of soil.

A stage border is the best of these three systems, because it allows more freedom of root action, but I realize that in some greenhouses in which there is a miscellaneous collection of plants, the pot or box method may be more convenient. Good crops are possible from both. Space the plants eighteen inches apart.

POLLINATION AND TRAINING

Tomato flowers are to some extent self-pollinated, but not sufficiently to guarantee a full set of fruit. Insects render very little help, for none of our British kinds seem interested in tomato flowers. It is, therefore, advantageous to pollinate the flowers by flicking them lightly each day with a feather duster, or a rabbit's tail attached to a stick. This simple attention may increased the yield by ten per cent.

In the early stages of growth remove the side shoots that form in the leaf joints with the point of a penknife blade, but after starting to gather the ripe fruit, a side shoot may be allowed to form and fruit in alternate leaf joints. In this way the yield is vastly increased. This is one of the new departures in tomato growing, and I specially recommend it to the notice of my readers. Tie the plants regularly to strings or wires fixed at intervals of a foot apart, and ten inches away from the glass. In the first stages of growth tie every four or five days. Progress is very rapid then, and if tying is deferred the stems will be broken in trying to pull them back to the wires.

DEFOLIATION

The tomato is a leafy plant, and so long as it makes the normal development of its species, the leaves are helpful. In them the food out of which the tomatoes are formed is manufactured. It will, therefore, be understood that extensive defoliation, or the removal of leaves,

A BUMPER CROP OF GREENHOUSE TOMATOES

is diametrically opposed to the interests of a good yield. Nobody should fall into that error.

At the same time defoliation may serve a useful purpose. When the plants become heavy with fruit, for example, the bottom leaves frequently go yellow and trail on the compost top. These leaves have fulfilled their function, and in trailing might be the means of conveying Botrytis or Stem Rot Disease to the plants. Cut them off, and if any of the upper leaves overhang a truss of fruit to such an extent as to impede ripening, cut them off also. Not many will do so, but it is as well to know that the elimination of any that obstruct in this way can be carried out. After removing the yellow or offending leaves, rub the cut end of the stem with a piece of liver of sulphur, to exclude disease spores.

TOP DRESSING AND FEEDING

As I indicated earlier, the minimum of compost is used at the beginning, to prevent souring. As growth goes forward, more of the mixture recommended for planting must be added. Fill up the pots and boxes by two-inch stages to within two inches of the top, and add two-inch layers to stage borders. Apply the first layer when roots show through the compost surface. That is a sign that the plants are ready for more help. Give successive layers as roots show through the previous one.

A recent change has come over conceptions regarding tomato feeding. It has been proved that if the plants are to bear good-sized top trusses, feeding must start early. They cannot do it otherwise. The time to begin (and this is a modification of much existing practice) is when the first fruits on the bottom truss are the size of a walnut. At intervals of five days from that stage until it is obviously no use feeding any more, give alternately quarter strength liquid manure (four pints per plant per time) and a mixture of three parts super-phosphate of lime and two parts sulphate of potash (one teaspoonful per plant per time). Sprinkle the fertilizer evenly on the soil around the main stem, and water it in. Of the many feeding schemes I have tried, none has given results equal to this. I would indicate that those who do not wish to go to the trouble of mixing their own food can buy excellent proprietary tomato feeding

compounds at the garden shop.   Use these in accordance
with the maker's instructions.

SHADING
The tomato is naturally a sun-loving plant, but in some
seasons, especially in lightly constructed houses, the plants
suffer slight embarrassment from continuous sunshine.
Their leaves become a pale green, which is a recognized
reaction to over-intense illumination.   When this occurs,
shade the glass lightly with thin whitewash, which must
be washed off when the conditions that cause the check
pass away.   In other words, shade as a regular factor
is to be deplored.   It is only permissible in special
circumstances.

TOMATOES IN PERMANENT BORDERS
Many amateur gardeners are now growing tomatoes
in permanent borders.   They build their greenhouse on
good land, and use this land for the cultivation of the
crop.   The idea is commendable from the yield and
labour-saving point of view.   It involves the double
digging of the border every Winter, without changing the
position of the spits or one foot layers.

When digging, mix with each square yard of bottom
spit a pailful of straw placed upright, and chopped into
six-inch long pieces.   Mix a similar quantity of well-rotted
manure with each square yard of top layer, and at least
twice during Winter give the border a thorough soaking,
using on each occasion fifteen gallons of water per square
yard.   A week before planting, having made the soil fine
and firm, rake in a two ounce per square yard helping
of a mixture of three parts superphosphate of lime and
two parts sulphate of potash.

Set the plants eighteen inches apart in blocks of five
rows, with a two feet wide path between each two blocks,
to allow for the necessary cultural attentions unless, of

course, the house is so small that there is no need for an arrangement of this kind. Provide a tightly stretched string for the support of each plant. In all other respects cultivation follows the lines above described.

A HEALTHY BATCH OF GROWING TOMATOES

SOIL STERILIZATION

This is a supremely vital process to which amateur gardeners should in their own interests give more careful attention. Tomatoes are subject to many root troubles, which arise through the activities in the soil of eelworms, harmful bacteria, protozoans, and the spores of diseases. Sterilization kills these foes. Without it, especially in permanent borders, the plants may be thoroughly disappointing, and unfortunately nothing can be done to help them. Anything that would kill the enemies would also kill the tomatoes. The sterilization must be carried out at least a month before seeds or plants go into the soil, to give the fumes from the sterilizer an opportunity to pass out.

The best chemical sterilizer is formaldehyde. Prepare it for use by stirring onè gallon into forty-nine gallons of water, and apply the solution to permanent borders at the rate of fifty gallons per twenty square yards. The border should be slightly moist when the application is made, and immediately after the application should be forked a foot deep. For forty-eight hours open the ventilators widely, to allow the fumes to escape. Borders cleansed in that way are ready for planting a month later.

Seed sowing, potting and planting composts should be sterilized with a similar solution, using two gallons per barrowful or one cwt. of compost. Sprinkle the mixture evenly through the heap from a rosed can, afterwards covering the heap with sacks for three weeks. The compost is ready for use one week after the sacks are removed.

Formaldehyde is not obtainable everywhere at the present time, but every year supplies can be obtained for sterilizing tomato composts and borders, on an official permit. Announcements regarding this permit are, at the appropriate periods, inserted in the gardening press.

One final word. If you have not already done so, join the army of sterilizers. Your success as a tomato grower depends on this. If you prefer not to use a crude chemical like formaldehyde, there are plenty of good proprietary preparations on the market.

Chapter III

TOMATO FOES

NO small part of success in tomato growing hangs on hygiene—keeping the environment clean, and the plants themselves free from pests and diseases. Of course, if hygiene receives its due share of attention, many of the pests and diseases will not attack, for there can be no doubt that these are in part transmitted from unclean surroundings.

WASHING DOWN THE HOUSE

To illustrate precisely what I mean, I would indicate that when the crop finishes each Autumn everything connected with it should, as far as possible, be removed from the house. Precede the cutting out of the plants by fumigating and spraying with a fungicide. Unless this is done, the disturbed pests and disease spores will find a harbour for the Winter, and reappear where they are not wanted the following Spring.

On removing the cut-down plants burn them, together with the strings that have been used to support the growth. Then wash down the house with a five per cent solution of cresylic acid, getting well into the corners. If there is litter in the pipe tracks, remove this and burn it also. Before starting operations each Spring, again wash down the house, this time with hot soapy water, and throughout

VERTICILLIUM WILT

(*By kind permission of Dr. Bewley, Director Cheshunt Experimental and Research Station*)

23

the season, when trimming the plants, cremate the side shoots and any unwanted growth. A general hygienic programme of this kind takes very little time, and is of priceless value in maintaining healthy plants. Now we are in a position to deal with specific enemies. Diseases are taken first.

SLEEPY DISEASE

This is due to a fungus which enters the root hairs, quickly passing to the thicker roots and the base of the stem. The ramifications of the enemy within the tissues intercepts the sap flow, causing the leaves to droop as if the plants required watering. Actually they do need moisture, but the means by which they can take it up are denied to them by the fungus. Eventually conditions become worse, and the plant dies.

As this disease is soil-borne, it follows that there must be a priceless advantage in planting in healthy soil, and this is done when the soil is sterilized as described in Chapter II, page 21. It is seldom that tomatoes growing in a sterilized medium fall victims to Sleepy Disease. We must, however, consider what to do when the roots are operating in unsterilized surroundings, and the disease invades.

Spraying with a fungicide is, of course, uesless since the enemy is both subterranean and internal, but happily the plants will, if action is taken early, recover by this treatment. Shade the glass over them, keep the soil markedly on the dry side, and spray overhead with clear water each day. After about a fortnight the plants will be able to hold out their leaves vigorously and normally, when the shading should be removed and orthodox treatment renewed. The dryness of the medium during the curative period destroys the fungus and induces the plants to form young roots.

CLADOSPORIUM DISEASE

Cladosporium Disease is also known as Rust and Mildew. It is, perhaps, the worst enemy of the tomato. Thousands of outbreaks that wreck crops would not occur if more attention were paid to atmospheric conditions. It can be assumed that the spores are in every greenhouse every Summer. If the relative humidity is allowed to

LEAF MOULD (CLADOSPORIUM FULCRUM)
Upper surface right   Lower surface left
(*By kind permission of Dr. Bewley, Director Cheshunt Experimental and Research Station*)

become more than ninety-five per cent, that is, almost moisture saturation, the spores will germinate, and an outbreak commence. I know there are cold, wet, dull spells during which the most careful use of water cannot keep down excess atmospheric humidity altogether, but more can and should be done by careful ventilation, and taking pains not to splash water about needlessly.

If the worst comes to the worst, and Cladosporium commences, the first symptoms will be yellow leaf blotches. These will increase in size and number, and ultimately the plants, fruit as well, will be covered with a brownish white felt of spores. When that stage is reached, the crop that might have been can no longer be. It lies in ruins at the grower's feet.

Action must follow speedily after an outbreak. Cut off and burn the infected leaflets, unless they are too numerous. Then spray with the standard preparation known as Shirlan Ag., which can be obtained at most garden shops. Choose a dull day or evening for the work, and that particular invasion will be mastered, though later in the season there can be a re-infection which will necessitate another spraying.

DAMPING OFF

This is a disease that attacks the seedlings while they are in the seed vessel for the most part. Occasionally an outbreak occurs in the first boxes into which they are transplanted. The responsible fungus works with the speed of lightning, destroying the seedlings and covering them with a white mould representing myriads of spores, every one of which can cause a fresh outbreak somewhere.

There is no cure for Damping Off. The attack is so forthright, and the seedlings so frail, that nothing can be done to save them. I am pleased, however, to say that there is in Cheshunt Compound a completely effective preventive. The seedlings should be watered with this Compound as soon as they appear, and every fortnight afterwards for eight weeks. Use a rosed can, and give as much of the solution as would be given of water if the plants were being watered normally.

Cheshunt Compound is made by mixing eleven parts by weight of carbonate of ammonia, and two parts by weight of powdered bluestone or sulphate of copper.

To prepare the solution, dissolve one ounce of this mixture in two gallons of water. A stock of Cheshunt Compound can be made up, for the preparation keeps well if stored in a tightly stoppered bottle or jar in a dry place.

Incidentally, if in the absence of this treatment Damping Off does arise, remove and burn the diseased seedlings. Spread dust charcoal or powdered brick on the vacant place, and put the remainder of the seedlings on to the Cheshunt Compound treatment immediately.

DAMPING OFF (PHYTOPHTHRON CRYPTOGEN)
(By kind permission of Dr. Bewley, Director Cheshunt Experimental and Research Station)

FOOT ROT DISEASE

The fungus that causes this trouble is closely akin to the one that is responsible for Damping Off, but it does not attack the seedlings until they are transplanted into boxes, and it may assail them at any time until they are thoroughly established in three and a half inch pots.

The point of attack is the base of the main stem, where the tissues dry up, causing the plants to topple over, never to rise again. Sometimes this disease is called Staggers, for obvious reasons. The Cheshunt Compound treatment advised as a safeguard against Damping Off is usually efficacious here, for in eight weeks after sowing the seedlings have acquired some vigour, and are able to resist the fungus unless they are badly checked by a fall in the temperature, or a cold draught striking them in a warm house.

For this reason I do not advise anything more as a routine operation than the Cheshunt Compound treatment for the first eight weeks. If there is an outbreak later, destroy the affected plants, and water the remainder once with Cheshunt Compound.

THE VIRUS DISEASES

The Virus Diseases are an infection of the sap. Scientists have not yet arrived at a definition of what a Virus is, but it is known that it is something so exceedingly minute that it will pass through a porcelain filter, the finest filter there is. If the significance of these viruses were relative to their size, we need not worry about them, but unfortunately there is no connection. The disorders caused by viruses constitute a problem to the tomato grower.

Problems, however, are there to be solved, and though nobody can be sure of escaping all the virus troubles, everybody can go a long way towards doing so by sowing the highest quality seed, and taking prompt action should the effect of a virus show in any of his plants. As these diseases can be seed-borne, the supreme necessity of getting the best seed will be obvious.

There are three really serious virus troubles. I will describe them in turn. The first is Bushy Head or Ferny Leaf, so called because in affected plants the number of leaf divisions is multiplied so enormously that these leaves resemble sometimes those of a fern, at others those of a pine tree. As this virus usually appears early, it is possible to eliminate and burn infected seedlings without making a gap in the permanent cropping arrangement. If, however, a plant that has started to crop should fall a victim to Ferny Leaf, pull it out and burn it.

The second virus is Mosaic Disease or Aucuba Leaf, so described because the leaves of stricken plants bear a yellow variegation similar to that revealed by the leaves of the shrub called aucuba. Watch for this trouble from the time the plants start to fruit, cut off and cremate the affected leaf or leaves, and the plant will, in all probability, recover. If events prove that the virus has spread too far, and there is an all-over mottling, the destruction of the plant is the only safe course.

The third virus is called the Distorting Virus, because it twists the leaves like a corkscrew. The fruit also is affected, developing on it yellow rings with a greenish centre like a bull's eye. Destroy affected plants promptly. It will be seen that there is no remedy for any of the viruses. The reason is that the virus is in the sap, and that no external application of any kind will touch it. It should be said that green-fly, a common greenhouse pest, is a serious spreader of virus, a good reason for getting rid of it on sight.

BLOSSOM END ROT

I refer to this in the chapter on tomato foes, but would make it clear that no fungus is responsible. The trouble, which is all too well known, reveals itself at the eye or flower end of the fruit, where sunken brown blotches appear. Ultimately these decay, due to the invasion of bacteria, but the primary cause is insufficient water. By that I do not mean that the plants concerned are not watered often enough. They may be, but the soil is not moistened right through, with the result that the cells in some part of the plant must be empty. It so happens that these emptied cells are found at the eye end of the fruit. They collapse and die. I need say no more. All that is needed to prevent Blossom End Rot is to water the plants thoroughly when they require moisture.

BLOSSOM END ROT
By kind permission of Dr. Bewley, Director Cheshunt Experimental and Research Station)

WARTY VEINS AND AERIAL ROOTS

Sometimes the veins in tomato leaves swell as if they were dropsical. Really they are, because they are distended with water. Sometimes also tufts of small roots or aerial roots push their way out of the stems. Neither of these abnormalities is caused by a fungus or bacterium. Both are due to excess atmospheric moisture, and will disappear if this is corrected by more liberal ventilation and less water splashing on the paths and stages.

WHITE-FLY

The White, Snowy, or Ghost Fly is the first of the insect pests with which I deal, because it is in most districts the most serious. The fly is like a small, snow-white midge, and the females of the species lay large numbers of eggs on the under surface of the leaves. There does not appear to be a clearly defined larval stage, but there are nymphs, which closely resemble this, and they, together with the adults, pierce the leaves and suck out the sap. The effect is most weakening.

Moreover, this pest deposits on the leaves a sticky secretion, on which ultimately a sooty mould develops, retarding respiration. Altogether, the effect of a heavy White-fly attack is very demoralizing. The pest is not difficult to exterminate if an outbreak is dealt with before egg-laying starts. The treatment consists in fumigating the house with one of the White-fly destroyers obtainable at the garden shop. Follow closely the instructions of the maker.

If no action is taken until eggs have been laid and nymphs hatched, it will be necessary to fumigate every five days until there are no more White-flies to be seen. Fumigation has no effect on the eggs and nymphs, hence these must be cleared up immediately they reach the adult stage.

RED SPIDER

In warm, sunny spells Red Spider can do a power of damage to tomatoes. This small red mite, which occurs in immense numbers on the leaves (usually on the under surface) extracts the sap to such an extent that the leaves become dry, brittle and pale yellow. Spraying forcibly with quassia extract solution (one part in eighty parts of water) destroys Red Spider. Being non-poisonous, this preparation can safely be used amongst food crops. I have previously stated that over-humidity is a frequent cause of Cladosporium. Now I must point out that under-humidity, or unnatural atmospheric dryness, is a cause of Red Spider attack. The happy medium is the best, and this can be attained by regulating the damping down of the paths in accordance with the weather.

THE TOMATO MOTH

The caterpillars of the Tomato Moth feed on both the fruit and the leaves. Attacked fruit quickly decays. These caterpillars are nocturnal feeders, hiding in the soil during the day. A visit to the house at twilight will discover them on their way to their feeding grounds and afford an opportunity of destroying them, which is the best control method known, so far as the caterpillars themselves go.

It is, however, better to prevent an attack by catching the moths, and this can be done by using the bait recommended by Dr. Bewley, the well-known tomato expert. It is as follows: Powdered malt extract four ounces, cheap ale one pint, sodium fluoride one quarter ounce. Mix the ingredients thoroughly, and divide the solution between eight jars, which should be hung up in the house. This bait has an irresistible attraction for the moths, which will meet their death in it.

GREEN-FLIES

Green-flies or aphides, those ubiquitous pests, are regular visitors to tomato houses, sucking the sap from the plants and, as I have previously pointed out, spreading virus diseases. Show no quarter to them. Dusting with the non-poisonous derris powder obtains the mastery if one is lucky enough to catch an infestation at its beginning. Should the pest have spread very much, fumigate the house on a calm night, thus making sure of exterminating every fly.

Directions for use are supplied with the excellent fumigants obtainable at the garden shop, but there may be amongst my readers those who would like to know how to measure the cubic capacity of their house. This is done by multiplying together the length, width and average height, all in feet. Thus, if a house is thirty feet long by ten feet wide, and has an average height of seven feet, the cubic capacity is as follows : $30 \times 10 \times 7 = 2,100$ cubic feet.

WIREWORMS

Wireworms, which at full development are yellow, hard-cased, inch-long grubs about the thickness of a match stalk, feed in the roots and main stems of tomato plants, destroying the tissues and stopping the sap flow. There is no doubt that sterilization of the composts and borders does something to control wireworms, but it certainly does not destroy them all. If it is found that these grubs are attacking, an excellent device is to impale small chunks of carrot or potato on pointed sticks, and bury the chunks at intervals of a foot or so in the compost or border. Examine the chunks each day, and destroy the wireworms that have collected on them. Further, it is advisable when preparing composts to search carefully for wireworms. If there are any they will be found in the turf, which is their natural home.

Chapter IV

LETTUCE IN THE HEATED GREENHOUSE

THE actual food value of lettuce is not high, but its health-giving value *is*. The crop is rich in vitamins, so much so that lettuce has been placed on the list of commercial glasshouse priority crops. Market gardeners are, under official orders, producing it in great volume in Winter and early Spring when, of course, there is no lettuce in the outdoor garden. I am sure amateur gardeners will desire to do their part in growing good, firm-hearted lettuce at these seasons.

CHOICE OF VARIETY

A glance through the average seed catalogue will show that there are numerous varieties of cabbage lettuce, the section on which we draw for greenhouse culture. Only a very few of these, however, are suitable for Winter and early Spring cultivation, because they possess the quality of forming firm hearts in the short days. The majority of sorts produce nothing more than blobs of leaves.

It will be appreciated, therefore, that considerable care must be exercised in selecting the variety. For my own part I have no hesitation in whittling the possibles down to two, namely, Cheshunt Early Giant and Loos Tennis Ball. The first-named is deep green, grows rather more quickly than Loos Tennis Ball, and forms a slightly larger heart. On the other hand, Loos Tennis Ball reveals that delicate, appetizing pale green which so many people like to see in lettuce. There is so little to choose between these two excellent sorts that either can safely be selected.

SOWING THE SEED

If seed is sown at three-weekly intervals from mid-September until mid-December, there will be an unbroken succession of lettuce from Christmas or thereabouts until the first of the cold frame batches is ready for cutting. When the cold frame lettuce is over, outdoor kinds will be ready, and the gardener is in a fair way for providing himself with an all-the-year-round supply of this valuable salad.

Use for sowing two and a half to three inch deep boxes, and a riddled compost of loam or turf three parts, leaf mould and sand one part each. Pass the two first-named ingredients through a half-inch sieve, to ensure an even texture. Use the rough riddlings for draining the boxes. After placing a half-inch layer of them at the bottom, fill up fairly firmly with compost to within half an inch of the top. Then level the surface, and kill weed seeds and other harmful compost occupants by watering through a rosed can with boiling water.

A GRAND LOT OF GREENHOUSE LETTUCE

As soon as the compost cools and drains, sow the seed very thinly, just cover it with silver sand, and place glass and brown paper over the boxes, these covers to remain, in the interests of stable germination conditions, until the seedlings show. As soon as they are visible, remove the covers, and stand the boxes on a light stage.

THE CARE OF THE SEEDLINGS

Scrupulously pure and slightly aired water must be used for watering greenhouse lettuce, which is soon inoculated with the root troubles that come from dirty water. It is possible with fair success to transplant straight from the seed boxes to permanent positions. Commercial growers do it to save time. It would be a colossal job dealing with the thousands of seedlings they need for their acres of glass.

The amateur gardener is, however, in a different category. He can spare the time to give those little extra attentions which mean bigger and firmer heads. That is why I advise transplanting young lettuce at two inches apart into other boxes when they have formed two or three normal leaves. The compost advised for seed sowing is appropriate, provided two ounces of a balanced fertilizer, such as National Growmore Fertilizer, are mixed with each pailful of the other ingredients. Water the seed boxes the day before lifting, to eliminate the risk of root injury. After transplanting, water carefully, and the crop will soon be ready for its final positions.

THE FINAL PLANTING

Here I must deal with two different sets of conditions. Many amateurs are now planting their tomatoes in permanent borders. Lettuce is an admirable follow-on crop. In fact, there is no better way of using these permanent borders between one season's tomatoes and those of another. I will deal with the planting of lettuce in these borders.

Before clearing the tomatoes fumigate the house, to destroy pests. After clearing them, wash it down with hot soapy water, stirring flowers of sulphur into this at the rate of an ounce to the gallon. Sulphur is a great destroyer of the fungi that cause diseases, hence its use in this connection. After clearing this crop, fork the borders a foot deep, without adding any organic manure. Before tomatoes are planted, the border is generously treated, and while the crop is fruiting it is well fed. The

36

residue of food left behind is quite sufficient to see the lettuce through. I stress that point, as it is possible to be too generous, with the result that the plants become super-succulent and unsatisfactory.

It is helpful to rake in superphosphate of lime at two ounces to the square yard, as this fertilizer firms the growth and promotes healthy root action. When forking remove the tomato roots, which in their fresh condition will not be difficult to extricate. Break down the lumps also, and tread moderately.

PLANT ON RIDGES

Growing lettuce, even in Winter, requires a good deal of water, but it is important that as little of this as possible shall splash the leaves, as dampness in that quarter causes Botrytis Disease. If the crop is planted on a level border, it is easy enough, while the plants are young, to water without wetting the foliage, but an obvious difficulty arises after they meet in the rows.

It is overcome by planting on six inch high ridges spaced eight inches apart. Whenever water is necessary it is poured into the furrows between the ridges, and does not at any time assume contact with the plants. The spacing on the ridges is eight inches also, and when planting it is a help to clip off a quarter of an inch to half an inch from the base of each tap root. This operation, though performed on a small plant, is the equivalent of root pruning a fruit tree. It induces the formation of surface fibrous roots, which keep growth sturdy and hasten the formation of nutty centres.

PLANTING IN BOXES

Those who have no permanent tomato borders will get very encouraging results if they grow their lettuce in four inch deep boxes. Bore holes at one foot apart hrough the bottom, to make sure that surplus water runs away quickly. As I indicated previously, lettuce is a great moisture lover, but if some of the water is held up and causes souring, the plants themselves will soon be little better than an apology for what they should be.

For this planting use a compost of loam or turf four parts, leaf mould, well-rotted manure and sand one part each, with two ounces of steamed bone meal to the pailful. Pass everything but the sand through a three-quarter inch sieve, and use an inch layer of the rough riddlings for drainage. Where stable manure is not obtainable, use as a substitute three ounces of prepared hop manure per pailful of the other ingredients. Plant eight inches apart, but leave the space for one plant vacant, so that water can be poured in there, afterwards making its way beneath the plants to all parts of the box.

THE TEMPERATURE

Hitherto I have not mentioned the temperature, because I wished to devote special consideration to this. I often feel that more tuition is needed on this important matter. Far too many gardeners set a datum or target, and keep to it under all circumstances. That is a great mistake with any crop. It is a serious mistake with lettuce. The temperature by fire heat in cold weather should be fifty degrees Fahr., in warm weather fifty-five degrees. Thus it will be seen conditions swing in sympathy with the weather.

If, for instance, the temperature is pushed up in cold weather, the plants will make to it the only response of which they are capable. They will grow more freely. Actually they will be forced into growth. The leaves will be over-sappy, will fall over and refuse to heart. That is the reason why the temperature should go down when outside conditions are imposing growth limitations.

If this point were more generally realized, there would be far greater success with greenhouse lettuce.

I am conscious of the fact that the sun will raise the temperature considerably, especially for the Spring batches. No apprehension need be felt about that. There is a great deal of difference between the type of heat produced by sunshine, and excessive heat engendered by artificial means. The former is life-giving, the latter takes away the conditions of a healthy life. Of course, when the sun is out the ventilators are opened a little more widely, to prevent scorching, but that is a point that will be considered later. What I am anxious to do now is to give a right lead on the maintenance of temperatures by artificial means.

LIGHT

That one word means a great deal. It is often said, and very truly, that water and light are the two primary needs of plant life. I have dealt with water as far as it concerns lettuce, now I touch on light. In Summer, when there is more daylight than darkness, nobody need worry very much about light. Provided lettuce is not sown in the shade, it receives plenty of it. But in Winter and early Spring conditions are vastly different.

In the depth of Winter there is not more than six or seven hours' effective daylight. This is a fact to which the would-be successful lettuce grower must give his attention. He must see to it that his crop receives full benefit of what light there is by standing boxes near the glass, and removing from houses in which there is a permanent border any obstacle which will interfere with the free access of light.

And it is most important that whenever a film of dirt settles on the glass the latter should be thoroughly washed. If the dirt is of a stubborn nature, a little washing soda dissolved in the water will remove it. Clearly the need for glass washing takes on a greater significance in urban areas, where so many amateurs' glasshouses are situated. It may be necessary under such conditions to wash these fortnightly.

VENTILATION AND FEEDING

There are no special points regarding the ventilation of greenhouse lettuce. It will be understood that there are days on which the ventilators must be closed completely. They should not be opened during severe frost, and it is imperative to have them very tightly closed during fog, the sulphurous fumes of which are damaging. If by any chance the greenhouse is leaky, the unofficial apertures should be stopped up during this period.

Though there are days on which ventilation is banned, there are more on which this is possible, and full use should be made of the opportunities to cleanse and vivify the atmosphere. Do not, however, permit cold draughts. Always open out on the leeward side, and regulate the amount of air strictly in accordance with the weather. It is by rescuing ourselves from stereotyped rule of thumb methods that we achieve our greatest triumphs. Nature is not mechanical, nor should those who look after her be so.

As I pointed out earlier, lettuce should not be over-fed, or it will go wasty. Nevertheless, a little assistance in the growing period is beneficial. It should take the form of two applications of sulphate of ammonia solution (one ounce per gallon of water, and one gallon per square yard of border or box space). Give the first application when the plants are half grown, the second one week later. That completes the purely cultivation programme, and I know from long experience that it will prove eminently satisfactory to those who practise it. I now turn to consider the enemies of lettuce, and a separate chapter will be devoted to these.

Chapter V

ENEMIES OF GREENHOUSE LETTUCE

BIRDS

BLUE-TITS and sparrows are very fond of lettuce. On attacking the plants they first remove the growing point, and thus make further progress impossible. These little creatures then proceed to tear the outer leaves to pieces. By some sort of knowledge which exists in the avian world, blue-tits and sparrows have got to know that lettuce is now extensively cultivated in greenhouses in Winter and Spring.

They make their way through the ventilators, and do an enormous amount of damage in a short time. Those who have a cat which has been trained to move about in the greenhouse without spoiling plants and knocking pots over, will find it an advantage to keep it on duty at the critical time. Birds will not enter if there is a cat on the watch, and if they do, they will soon be caught. Where this expedient cannot be practised, there is no alternative to that of spreading small mesh wire or cotton tan netting in front of the ventilators, thus making it physically impossible for the birds to gain admittance.

GREEN-FLY

Green-fly is the worst enemy of lettuce under glass. If it did no more damage than that of sucking sap, its attentions would be deplorable. But it does. This pest turns in with the heart leaves, fouls them, and makes the lettuce quite unfit to eat. This method of feeding renders it imperative to keep a sharp look-out for the appearance of the pest. The plants should be examined every four or five days, and if but one green-fly is seen, do not think that it is of no account. There are sure to be others somewhere in the offing. Get rid of the enemy by dusting twice with derris powder, the second application to be four days after the first. Where, owing to the number of the plants, or the extent of the infestation, this operation would prove too onerous, fumigate the house on a calm night.

WIREWORMS

Wireworms are occasionally troublesome to lettuce. These yellow, hard-cased grubs are inhabitants of the soil, from which they make their way into the butt or short main stem, where they feed and interrupt the sap flow. In consequence the plants droop, and in most cases perish. The best way to clear up an infestation of this type is to bury small pieces of carrot or potato in marked places, examine them daily, and destroy the wireworms that will collect to feed on them. Keep these traps going as long as they catch anything. When they cease to do so, it can safely be assumed that the menace is cleared up.

THE ROOT APHIS

This subterranean, wingless, white wool-covered insect is akin to the green-fly. It clusters on the roots of lettuce, and withdraws sap from them. The plants reveal their discomfiture by going sluggish and lustreless. Happily the pest is not difficult to master, as will be proved if the border or boxes are watered with permanganate of potash solution (one quarter ounce in two gallons of water, and two pints per plant). Incidentally, there is in this solution a food which assists the lettuce to recover quickly.

BOTRYTIS DISEASE

This disease, which is also called " water-soak," can do irreparable damage to the crop. It begins by forming damp brown blotches in the leaves. These enlarge and increase in number. As the leaves are the edible part, it follows that corrective measures must be undertaken promptly.

Formerly it was the custom to apply a copper lime dust, but there were objections. Firstly, none of these dusts were really effective. Secondly, they tainted the flavour of the lettuce. Now it is considered by far the best policy to cut out the affected parts with sharp scissors, preferably nail scissors, which make a very precise cut, and burn them. It must be made clear that overhead watering, or drips from a leaky roof, are predisposing causes of Botrytis. Neither should be tolerated where lettuce is.

DOWNY MILDEW

A disease that is very liable to break out when the weather is persistently damp and sunless. The fungus responsible covers the under surface of the leaves with a purplish-white down. The effect is very weakening. Dusting with green sulphur powder is a certain remedy.

STEM CANKER

This disease attacks the butt or short main stem, causing the tissues to dry up. As sap cannot pass the diseased part, affected plants have no alternative but to droop and die. There is no cure, for once the sap passages are destroyed, nothing can replace them. But Canker rarely occurs in well drained boxes or borders, hence the necessity for attending carefully to drainage. Should there be a mild outbreak pull up and burn diseased plants, and spread a half-inch layer of sand on the border to ensure those dry surface conditions in which it is impossible for the Canker fungus to flourish.

Chapter VI

MELONS, CUCUMBERS, VEGETABLE MARROWS AND SQUASHES

THERE are many cultural requirements common to melons, cucumbers, vegetable marrows and squashes, but as it is never very helpful reading about several subjects at the same time, because there are points of difference which must be sorted out, I propose to deal with the subjects separately, beginning with melons.

These are amongst the most delicious fruits in cultivation. There can be nothing much more refreshing than the experience of partaking of a well-ripened melon on a warm, summery day. All that under such conditions is needed to make a man or woman perfectly happy is a victory on the golf course or tennis court.

SEED SOWING AND VARIETIES

Sow the seed separately some time between early January and the middle of May in clean, well drained three-inch pots filled to within one-third of an inch of the top with a sifted compost of loam or turf three parts, leaf mould and sand one part each. If the seed is pressed in edgeways one quarter of an inch to half an inch deep, the seed skins will remain in the compost, thus preventing that deformity which so frequently hinders the progress of young melons.

After sowing, stand the pots in a box, without watering, on the hot water pipes. The seedlings will be through in little more than twenty-four hours. They are always more vigorous when they are germinated under these intensively warm conditions. The following are most reliable kinds : white-fleshed, Hero of Lockinge ; scarlet-fleshed, Blenheim Orange ; green-fleshed, Delicatesse.

THE CARE OF THE SEEDLINGS

It is a matter of great significance that the seedlings should not only be kept growing, but should grow rapidly. A check caused by a draught, a violent change of temperature, watering with cold or impure water, is enough to hold up growth and play havoc with the chances of obtaining a good crop.

Watch these points, therefore, and if it is not possible to transfer the plants to their permanent quarters before they become root-bound, move them into five inch pots, adding one part of well-rotted manure to the compost advised for seed sowing. In a root-bound state melon plants become hard-stemmed and small-leaved. They lose their fruiting bias. When watering, be most careful not to splash the stems, or Canker will result.

THE FINAL PLANTING

If I could choose, I would plant my melons in a nine inch wide, six inch high, flat-topped border on the greenhouse stage, as near to the side glass as possible, fixing ten inches away from the glass strings or wires to support the growth. There is a freer root range in a border, and the melons are happier for it.

They can, however, be successfully grown in nine-inch pots, or boxes of similar size, both of which should in the beginning be half-filled only. Later in the season top dressings must be given in these receptacles as well as to a continuous stage border.

The best stage at which to transplant to these quarters is when the fifth or sixth leaf has been formed. Growth is then young, supple and vigorous—excellent qualities which it never loses. The day before planting, water the young melons to avoid the root injury which will follow if the plants are knocked out of their pots dry. Do not disturb the soil ball any more than is necessary, plant firmly, and for a time water with caution. After growth gets going, abundant supplies of moisture are essential.

THE CORDON SYSTEM

I did not, when dealing with the final planting, give the spacing, because this is governed by the system of training. It is a fact that no melon plant can bear the strain of carrying more than four fruits. Often it is difficult to secure these, for if one fruit gets a lead of the others, the latter will just go yellow and perish. As one cannot control the development rate, disappointments of this nature are not infrequent.

For that reason I prefer the cordon system, and one fruit per plant. It absolves one from the anxiety dependent on watching the fruits develop, and ensures a better yield. Where this method is decided on, set the plants a foot apart. After planting, allow each plant to grow seven or eight feet before taking out the growing point. As a result of doing so, a side shoot will develop from practically every leaf joint. Each will bear both male and female flowers. The latter must be pollinated, as there are no other means whereby the pollen can be transferred.

THE POLLINATION OF MELONS

The female flowers are easily recognized by the tiny embryonic fruit beneath the petals. The male blooms have no fruit beneath their petals, but in other respects are similar. They carry the pollen, and it is this which must be transferred. To do so nip off a flower, take away the petals carefully and push the exposed yellow central core into the centre of the female bloom, leaving it there for Nature in her own way to complete the process of fertilization. Pollination is merely the mechanical act of transferring the pollen. Fertilization follows that.

Transfer the pollen as near midday as can be arranged, for at that hour it is in its most potent condition. And pollinate several flowers on one plant at the same time, reducing the resulting fruits to one per plant when they are about the size of a tennis ball.

46

Take out the growing point of the bearing shoot two leaves beyond the safely swelling fruit, and remove that of the other side shoots and resulting sub-laterals when they have formed their fifth leaf. In this way growth is restrained, and there is no overcrowding. As melons are fairly heavy and the growth is very succulent, it is essential to support the fruits, and this should be done before there is any sagging. Special melon nets can be bought for a few coppers each. They are slung to the supports like a hammock, and the fruits rest in them without any bruising. Where for any reason nets are not used, two strands of raffia or tape per fruit answer well. They must be tied underneath the fruit, and also to the nearest firm support.

THE TEMPERATURE

The melon is the most tropical fruit produced in British glasshouses. For that reason the most successful results are obtained in a high temperature. Where it can be arranged, nothing less than seventy-five degrees Fahr. should be permitted from beginning to end. It is possible, however, to grow nice fruit in a temperature of sixty-eight to seventy degrees.

Naturally, with such a high thermometer reading, the atmosphere is liable to get very dry and unhealthy unless the path and stages are damped down two or three times on warm, bright days, and as many times as are considered necessary on dull, cool ones. Ventilation should be on a modest scale—just sufficient to prevent sun-scorch. Naturally, when there is humidity in the house, ventilation on these restricted lines will create the Turkish bath atmosphere which melons like so much.

FEEDING AND RIPENING

From the time the fruits are the size of a tennis ball until they start to ripen, feed every five days with quarter strength liquid manure, giving each plant one gallon per dose. Soluble dried blood (one ounce per gallon of water, and six pints per plant per application) may be used as a substitute.

As soon as the fruits commence to ripen, suspend feeding, and reduce watering to the minimum consistent with keeping the leaves fresh. Give a little more air, too. Under these conditions the fruits will soon be completely ripe, when the cultivator can proceed to enjoy the results of his labour.

TOP DRESSING CUCUMBERS

THE ALTERNATIVE METHOD

The alternative training method consists in spacing the plants three feet apart and securing, or endeavouring to secure, four fruits per plant. To this end remove the growing point immediately above the fifth leaf, and that of the resulting side shoots above the fifth leaf also. The numerous sub-laterals that now form will rapidly unfold male and female blooms. Pollinate a good number of these simultaneously, and thin the resulting fruitlets to four per plant when they are the size of a tennis ball.

It is obviously an advantage to space the retained fruits more or less evenly, and as far apart as possible. Take out the growing point of the bearing shoots two leaves beyond the fruit, and that of the non-bearers just above the fifth leaf. In other respects the management programme is similar to that already described, but as I have indicated, there may be losses due to uneven swelling.

CUCUMBERS

There are very few points of difference between the cultivation of cucumbers on the branching system outlined immediately above, and that of melons. I will now mention these differences. Firstly, the temperature need not be quite as high. Good cucumbers of a variety like Conqueror can be grown well in a temperature of sixty to sixty-five degrees Fahr. Where it is possible to run greater heat, seventy to seventy-five degrees is the ideal, and a good strain of Telegraph or Butcher's Disease Resisting cannot be beaten.

The plants produce male and female flowers, but the females must not on any account be pollinated, or they will develop a large number of seeds and become what expert growers call bull-necked. Such cucumbers are quite useless unless one is producing seed, and very few people grow the crop for that purpose. In order to prevent occasional natural pollination, it is a good plan to remove the male blooms. Where this is not done, bull-necked fruits that do appear must be destroyed.

There is, of course, no ripening in the case of cucumbers. On the contrary, it is wise to keep well up to the cutting, never allowing any fruit to form a skin so hard that the thumb-nail cannot be pushed through it.

This is in the interests not only of continued production, but of pleasure to the consumer. In other respects cucumbers should be treated as I have described for melons. They can, where the necessary temperatures exist, be grown all the year round, though it is customary to sow from January to June, as in these months the yields are heavier.

CUCUMBERS IN THE GREENHOUSE

VEGETABLE MARROWS AND SQUASHES

Vegetable marrows and squashes are primarily outdoor crops, but many people who have a heated greenhouse like to raise them early, and very choice they are. The sowing months are January to March, and the plants are trained as advised for the branching system in melon growing. There is no need to restrict the number of fruits per plant. Allow each plant to carry as many fruits as it will. Usually production is very heavy.

In these cases the female flowers must be pollinated as they open. Young fruits will not yellow if there are other fruits ahead of them. Non-success frequently follows pollination because flowers at an unsuitable stage

VEGETABLE MARROWS IN THE GREENHOUSE

are used. Both the male and the female are at the best for discharging their respective functions when they are one day old.

The fruits should be supported as I advise for melons, but the same cutting test applies as for cucumbers. Do not allow the skins to harden, or the marrows and squashes will be past their best from the culinary point of view. Two very choice vegetable marrows for greenhouse work are Rotherside Orange and Moore's Cream.

Perhaps a little explanation concerning squashes would be appreciated. They are closely allied to vegetable marrows, and though there are many types the Hubbard squash, with its lemon-shaped fruits, is the one most frequently grown, and it certainly justifies its popularity because of the choice flavour. The fruits can be cooked like those of the marrow, or made into that excellent dish, squash pie. The ideal temperature for these two crops is sixty-five degrees Fahr., and in all respects save those mentioned the melon programme is appropriate.

Chapter VII

ENEMIES OF MELONS, CUCUMBERS, VEGETABLE MARROWS AND SQUASHES

HOW TO CONTROL THEM

MELONS, cucumbers, vegetable marrows and squashes are liable to be attacked by several enemies. Most of them are common to the four crops. Where an enemy is peculiar to one of the four, or to a special set of conditions, I will mention these. Otherwise my observations can be taken to apply equally to melons, cucumbers, vegetable marrows and squashes.

EELWORMS

Eelworms are almost microscopic worms which attack the crops under glass. They invade the roots, causing the formation of small, bladder-like swellings, which actually are packed with these parasites. Growth becomes stunted, and cropping ceases. In fact, it is difficult to imagine an enemy which more effectively completes its fell work of destruction.

There is no remedy, as any preparation which is applied to the soil with crops growing in it will, if it kills the eelworms, prove fatal to the crop itself. If an infestation is caught very early, the eelworms are prevented from multiplying by drenching the soil with permanganate of potash solution (one quarter of an ounce in two gallons of water).

The gardener's real salvation, however, is to grow these crops in soil which has been sterilized in accordance with the method described in Chapter II, page 21. Sterilization does destroy the eelworms, and if the composts are free from them, there is no fear of an attack.

THE TURNIP FLEA BEETLE

In recent years the Turnip Flea Beetle, a small brightly-coloured insect which pits and punctures the seed leaves and first true leaves of radishes, turnips, and members of the cabbage family, has added to its food range by including young greenhouse marrows, cucumbers and squashes. No attack has yet been recorded on melons. The effect on the fleshy seed leaves is so deadly that the seedlings, which should grow very rapidly, develop slowly and weakly. Happily this pest can be destroyed by dusting with derris powder before the leaves dry after overhead spraying. The powder lies closely on a moist surface, and does its good work well.

RED SPIDER

This is a very serious foe, especially on cucumbers and melons. Though the tiny red mites measure no more than one-fiftieth of an inch in length, they multiply at such an exceedingly rapid rate that very soon there are literally thousands on one infested plant. The mites live by sucking sap, and so thoroughly do they operate that in a short time the leaves are almost as much bleached as if they had been soaked in alcohol. It goes without saying that every normal function is deranged, and the net result is complete failure.

Much can be done to prevent an attack of Red Spider by maintaining a pleasantly humid atmosphere, by carefully regulated overhead spraying with clear water, and damping down the paths and walls. A further valuable deterrent influence is exercised by the smell of ammonia which will be generated perpetually in the house if the evaporizing troughs on the pipes are kept filled with quarter strength liquid manure.

If for any reason an attack should develop, spray with quassia extract solution immediately it is observed, and the enemy will be destroyed. Fumigation with naphthalene has been tried with success, but I do not advise the amateur to liberate this gas in his greenhouse.

THE THRIPS INSECT

The black Thrips insect and its yellow larvæ adopt the same feeding method as red spiders, and multiply rapidly under similar atmospheric conditions. All that I have said about the control of red spider applies equally to thrips, with the one added reservation that spraying with the quassia extract solution must be very forcibly done, as thrips find their way into leaf crevices, which can only be reached by a forcibly ejected spray.

WOOD-LICE

Wood-lice, slaters or pillboxes, as these enemies are called, can do serious damage by gnawing through the base of the main stems. They are always more troublesome in old greenhouses, in which they find acceptable shelter in the decaying wood. They also breed and harbour beneath the litter which is so often thrown into the pipe track. This practice is to be deplored, and where there is any litter I suggest that it should be cleared up, so that the wood-lice may be driven into the open.

A wood-louse poison which is non-poisonous to human beings is a mixture of equal parts of dried blood and pyrethrum powder. The latter is the poison, the former the bait; and as wood-lice cannot resist dried blood, they soon meet their doom if small heaps of the mixture are laid about the house.

A simple and effective trap is made by cutting lengthways good-sized potatoes, scooping out most of the flesh and laying the scooped-out portions concave side downwards in the wood-louse haunts. The creatures collect in them, and the haul should each day be destroyed.

FRUIT ROT DISEASE

Very frequently young cucumbers, melons, marrows and squashes start to rot from the flower end, the decay proceeding rapidly until there is nothing left but mush. Many gardeners believe that this is due to non-pollination, but that is not so. A female flower that is not pollinated (cucumbers excepted) shrivels and dries up. There is none of the wet rot about it that is associated with Fruit Rot Disease. The enemy here is a fungus, and it spreads so speedily that every fruit that is formed may become a victim.

The remedy is to spray with liver of sulphur solution (one ounce in three gallons of water), adding to the solution one of the proprietary spreaders in accordance with the maker's instructions, to ensure an even coverage. In addition, destroy all infected fruits. In this, as in so many other instances, we find that an enemy visitation is assisted by unpropitious atmospheric conditions. Fruit Rot is almost sure to appear if the air is over-saturated with moisture. Gardeners soon learn when the right balance is struck, and this should be the aim with the four crops that form the subject of our immediate discussion.

STEM CANKER

This is a disease that attacks the base of the stems, causing the tissues there to turn brown and dry up. The part above the disease lesion perishes, because the roots are unable to send any sap to it. No remedy is known, for unfortunately as soon as Stem Canker has progressed far enough to be observed, it has gone too far for any curative treatment to be applied. This does not mean that the disease is one to be feared very much, because if the plants are kindly treated there will be no outbreak.

Cold and impure water must not, for instance, be used, and when watering with pure water it is essential not to splash the stems. This can be avoided if a cordon of hazel nut sized pieces of lime rubble or charcoal is built round each stem.

MOSAIC DISEASE

While the four crops are susceptible to attack by the virus causing Mosaic Disease, cucumbers are most so. The symptoms of infection are a yellow leaf variegation, a stunted habit, and sterility. If as soon as the variegation is observed the shoot bearing the affected leaves is cut out and burned, it is very unlikely that there will be further trouble. In the odd case in which there is an almost universal outbreak simultaneously, the best course is to pull up and burn the entire plant, for as I have already explained, nobody has yet discovered a spray that will overcome a virus in the sap. As this trouble can be spread on the seed coat, it is most important to buy only the best seed.

MILDEW

Mildew is due to the activities of a parasitic fungus which pushes suckers into the leaves, and extracts sap from them. The mealy appearance of infected plants is well-known, for Mildew is one of the commonest troubles. Cold draughts, violent temperature changes, and a moisture-sodden atmosphere are pre-disposing causes that should be avoided. If there should be an outbreak, it can be got under by dusting with green sulphur powder or flowers of sulphur.

LEAF SPOT

This disease attacks cucumbers and melons, the first symptoms being the appearance of small pale green leaf blotches. These gradually enlarge, turn greyish-brown, and may ultimately fall out. As the leaf surface is the cucumber and melon manufacturing department, it follows that an infection of this type is going to reduce cropping capacity.

So it does, and very quickly too. Draughts, watering with ice-cold water, and quick temperature changes render the crops more prone to attack, but even where every precaution is taken there is no guarantee against an outbreak, which can be controlled by spraying with liver of sulphur solution as advised for Foot Rot Disease. Where the outbreak starts in a small number of leaves, as it usually does, these can, with advantage to the control campaign, be cut off and burned.

Chapter VIII

POD-BEARING CROPS

FRENCH BEANS are a great delicacy in Winter and Spring. Where a succession is desired, the sowings should be at three-weekly intervals from mid-November to mid-February. Varieties that do specially well under glass are Lightning and The Prince. An ideal temperature is sixty-five to seventy degrees Fahr. If the thermometer falls below this, there is a danger that the flowers may drop prematurely, or the pods turn yellow.

HOW TO SOW

Clean eight-inch pots are the best growing receptacles, for they have porous sides, but excellent results can be obtained in boxes of similar depth. Drain the pots and boxes with a single layer of clean inverted crocks or potsherds, just covering them with walnut-sized pieces of turf. Unless there is a small opening between the bottom boards in the boxes, holes should be bored at nine inches apart to allow for the escape of superfluous water.

Having completed this drainage scheme, half fill the pots or boxes with a mixture of loam three parts, leaf mould, well-rotted manure and sand one part each. The plants will grow and crop well spaced five inches apart, but as one cannot be sure that every seed will germinate, it is advisable to sow a few extra seeds, pulling up the redundant seedlings later if there is a full germination.

After sowing, stand the pots on a light stage, but do not water until the seedlings show, unless the compost dries out unduly. In the early stages water cautiously, but freely, when the plants have formed seven or eight leaves.

ATMOSPHERIC CONDITIONS

French beans enjoy a pleasantly humid atmosphere, but as the season is Winter and early Spring, the establishment of this needs most careful thought. It would, for instance, on a dark Winter day be mightily indiscreet to spray the plants overhead with water, but they would enjoy such an experience on a bright February day. When the air outside hangs heavy with moisture, the

SOWING PEAS IN BOXES

atmosphere in a heated greenhouse, however weather-proof the structure may be, tends to be similar, and very little damping down is needed to get the right degree of humidity.

It is by damping down and overhead spraying that these conditions are provided, and it is also for the gardener himself to decide how much of either he will require to make his French beans happy. That is a point I would like to make. Do not adopt a hard and fast rule, but let an acute and ever-active judgment decide.

STAKING AND FEEDING

The crop invariably needs a little support. Where light twigs are available, these can be used. Just sufficient of them to hold the growth up, not making a thicket through which light cannot penetrate. Stakes and string are a satisfactory alternative to twigs.

PEAS GROWING IN A GREENHOUSE BORDER

As soon as the first flowers open, fill up the pots or boxes to within one and a half inches of the top with the compost advised for sowing. This compost should be warmed by standing in the house for three or four days before it is used. Top dressing is, of course, an act of feeding, but is not enough. Supplement it by five-day applications of quarter strength liquid manure or soluble dried blood (half an ounce to the gallon of water) from the time when the first pods are three inches long until the crop is finished.

GREENHOUSE GREEN PEAS READY FOR GATHERING

THE GUERNSEY RUNNER

Though this variety is called a runner, it is in reality a climbing French bean, reaching five feet tall. Where there is head room, it gives heavier yields than the dwarf French beans, for the simple reason that it fills up space which they do not.

I recommend the variety to all who have the necessary conditions. The cultural programme generally is similar. There is a difference in the method of sowing. One seed should be set in a three and a half inch pot, and the resulting seedling should be transferred to a seven-inch pot before it becomes root-bound. Provide for each plant a five feet tall stake, around which it will twine.

BROAD BEANS

Excellent crops of broad beans can be obtained in a greenhouse in April and May from a November sowing. The variety Giant Windsor is most reliable. The great point to remember is that the temperature should not exceed fifty degrees Fahr. at any time. Too much heat will make the plants so spindly and succulent that they will not bear a pod.

The seed should be sown in precisely the manner advised for French beans, top dressing when the plants show bloom. As growth develops, support each plant with a stake, and when basal side shoots form rub them off with the finger and thumb. As soon as the plants have set six good pods, take out the growing point of each, and until the pods are full feed every week with superphosphate of lime (one teaspoonful per pot per dose). Regulate the quantity in boxes according to the size of the box, and in each case water the fertilizer in.

PEAS

Good supplies of peas can be had in April from December sowings, and though many varieties do well, I have not found any to equal the eighteen inch tall Peter Pan. Space the seed three inches apart, and bury it half an inch deep. Eight-inch pots or boxes may be used. Support each plant with a stake, and give abundant light and plenty of fresh air. The slightest shade causes the flowers to go blind.

HEALTHY BROAD BEANS IN BOXES

Each plant should bear twelve pods, and as soon as these have set remove the growing points, as well as any side shoots that may subsequently arise. After the first pods are set, feed precisely as advised for broad beans.

Chapter IX

ENEMIES OF POD-BEARING CROPS

POD-BEARING crops under glass are liable to be embarrassed by enemies similar to those which attack these vegetables out of doors. If success is to be attained, it is necessary to gain the upper hand, for no crop can do well if embarrassed by an insect or fungal parasite. I will consider first the foes of French beans.

RED SPIDER

This small red mite so often attacks French beans that it may almost be considered a hereditary enemy of the crop. The effect of the greedy sap-sucking is to rob the plant of vitality, and by depriving it of chlorophyll or green colouring matter to prevent it from replacing the nutriment that has been lost. It is inevitable on this account that when French beans fall thoroughly into the grip of Red Spider, they go the wrong way very quickly.

The mite flourishes best in a dry atmosphere, hence the maintenance of a humid air by overhead syringing and damping down is a first-class safeguard. Indeed, if there is faithfulness in the maintenance of these conditions, Red Spider will not get the proverbial look-in.

We are all human, however, and sometimes, in spite of resolutions to the contrary, we fall from grace and the enemy gets in. Whenever he does, he can be destroyed by forcible spraying with the non-poisonous quassia extract solution. Needless to say, action should be taken promptly, for after Red Spiders spin their protective webs eradication is more difficult.

SLUGS

The Slug pest in a humid greenhouse may assume rather serious proportions. These slimy creatures hide in the stage breeze, emerging at night to do their destructive work. A fair-sized black or grey Slug can eat through the stem of a French bean seedling between darkness and dawn. If it does, of course, that is the end. Should the attack develop later, the slugs riddle the leaves and eat chunks out of the pods. Altogether slugs are thoroughly undesirable.

Much can be done to dispose of them by searching and hand picking, and too much praise cannot be bestowed on the metaldehyde fuel traps. Bars of metaldehyde can be bought at the garden shop. Crush them to powder, and mix one ounce of this with three pounds of bran or bone meal. In war-time, when bran cannot be used, bone meal makes an excellent substitute. Set small heaps of this mixture about the greenhouse, and the slugs will be found where everyone likes to see them—stretched out dead near the irresistible bait which they have taken.

GREEN-FLY

Green-fly is common to French and broad beans and peas. My observations, therefore, in this case apply to the three crops. Amazing as is the rate of increase out of doors, it is nothing to be compared with that which takes place in the stable conditions of a warm greenhouse. In a very short time after an attack begins, the plants literally heave with these disgusting and destructive lice. Spraying with quassia extract solution or derris wash is a certain remedy if all the insects are wetted, but there are so many corners about a plant that to find them all with a spray is very difficult. That is why I am in favour of fumigation, which finds and exterminates every fly.

MICE

There are few greenhouses which are not occasionally invaded by mice. As everyone knows, these little rodents have a particular affection for the seeds of pod-bearing crops, which they mark down and consume. They also empty the pods of broad beans and peas, and sometimes clear pea pods from plants, storing them in a convenient larder. Happily mice are in the main simple creatures which can easily be trapped. If they prove too old-fashioned to go into these, spread some poison on bits of cheese laid about the house. This will disarm their suspicion, and very soon there will be an end of the menace.

HALO BLIGHT

This is a disease peculiar to French beans, attacking the leaves and pods. The external symptoms of infection are small pale yellow circles in the leaves and pods, each circle having a dark green centre. The effect is something like that of the bull's-eye in a shooting target. The gardener can, however, soon see that there is nothing either interesting or ornamental about Halo Blight, for the affected parts of the pods and leaves cease to grow, while the intermediate parts continue to grow in the best way they can. Very distorted organs result. Flowers fail to set after Halo Blight makes its appearance, and generally the crop has to be written off as something that might have been.

As this disease may be seed-borne, and the marks of it can be seen on the seed coat, it is a wise practice to examine the seed for them, rejecting any that show the disease. The tell-tale marks are small, pimply scabs. Do not soak the seed before sowing, as it has been proved that seed submitted to this treatment is much more susceptible to infection. Grow the plants in a clean greenhouse, on the principle that disease always follows dirt. If these precautions are followed, there is more than a sporting chance of immunity, but if Halo Blight develops, get to grips with it promptly, cutting off and burning the diseased parts, and spraying with liver of sulphur solution (one ounce in three gallons of water). Use a proprietary spreader, obtainable at any garden shop, to ensure a good coverage of the solution.

BLACK ROOT ROT

Black Root Rot attacks French and broad beans and peas, and may occur at any stage of growth. The spores may be air-borne or soil-borne, usually the latter, a powerful argument for sterilizing the compost as advised in Chapter II, page 21. The first indications that anything is wrong are a loss of the green colour associated with perfect health, and the emergence of a black blotch at the base of the stem. On examination it is found that the roots are affected too.

There is no cure for this disease if it proceeds very far before action is taken. Affected plants should be burned. If, however, the trouble is detected early, and each diseased plant is watered with two pints of permanganate of potash solution (one quarter of an ounce of the crystals in two gallons of water), it will invariably recover.

BLACK-FLY

The Black Dolphin or Black-fly, a wingless sap-sucking insect, confines its attentions to broad beans, and it only attacks these when Spring is pretty far advanced. The relationship between Green and Black-fly is so close that it is only the colour of the skin which separates the two species. Black-fly multiplies as quickly as green-fly, and early fumigation is the best way of dealing with it.

CHOCOLATE SPOT DISEASE

Broad beans are the sole sufferers in this case. The first symptoms, which are not alarming, are the appearance on the leaves of small pin-point-sized spots. As these represent the activities of a parasitic fungus, the internal effect is more serious than the outward signs denote.

This will be realized if the specks are allowed to increase so much that they cover practically the entire plant. All hopes of a crop will then disappear rapidly.

There is no doubt that a clammy, oppressive atmosphere is responsible for the initiation of many an outbreak of Chocolate Spot Disease, but even when a brisk and buoyant atmosphere is maintained, it does not follow that the crop will escape. Should it fall a victim, spray with liver of sulphur solution, as advised for Halo Blight Disease.

LEAF-EATING WEEVIL

A Leaf-eating Weevil occasionally infests broad beans and peas, snipping semi-circular pieces out of the leaf margins. As every bit of leaf surface is valuable, particularly in the dark months when these crops are grown under glass, it is only to be expected that when weevils feed on broad beans and peas the crops go by default.

The origin of the attack is often a mystery, for the pest is a night feeder, hiding in the soil during the day. The best way to destroy it is to sprinkle a little lime on the leaves and the soil as well.

SEED-EATING WEEVILS

The same Weevil that feeds on the leaves of broad beans and peas may also tunnel into the seeds. Another Weevil is guilty of doing this also. Clear evidence exists of the presence of one or both in the tiny holes by which the insects have entered. As these invaders are living on the embryonic plant, they are in a position to do irreparable damage. Should their presence be detected at seed-time, empty the seed into a box, treat it with carbon bisulphide, and close the box for twenty-four hours. At the end of that time every Weevil will be destroyed. Use the chemical at the rate of half an ounce to a pint of seed, and do not bring it near a naked light, as carbon bisulphide is very inflammable.

PEA MILDEW

The time of the year at which glasshouse peas are grown, with its defective light and cold days, makes peas susceptible to Mildew, a disease which covers the leaves, pods and flowers with a dirty white, mealy down. The risk of attack is considerably lessened by avoiding cold draughts, an over-wet soil, and too much moisture in the atmosphere. Should there be an outbreak, get rid of it expeditiously by dusting with a mixture of two parts flowers of sulphur and one part lime.

Chapter X

MISCELLANEOUS CROPS

SEVERAL useful crops can be grown in boxes in the heated greenhouse, and one great advantage of these is that they are easily moved about. They can go on to the shelf or stage, in accordance with the lay-out of the house.

PREPARATION OF THE BOXES

It is not advisable to restrict the crops for rooting space, nor yet is it advisable to give them too large a body of soil, which becomes over-wet and sour. I suggest the four inch deep, twelve inch wide, two feet long box. The length and width are not very important, but it is helpful to go in for uniformity, thus making it possible to pack the boxes on the stage without wasting space. It is also prudent to remember that a large box is heavy when full of damp soil, and may collapse by its own weight.

An ideal general compost is a mixture of loam or sods three parts, leaf mould, well decayed manure and sand one part each. Pass the ingredients through a half-inch sieve, to ensure an even texture. If it is impossible to obtain stable manure, use as a substitute three ounces of prepared hop manure per pailful of the other ingredients.

DELICIOUS RADISHES GROWN IN THE GREENHOUSE

In this book I have consistently advised compost sterilization. I mention that process again, because of its obvious advantages. Drain each box with an inch layer of the rough riddlings, afterwards filling up the boxes with compost to within three-quarters of an inch of the top. Level the surface with a flat board, and the boxes are ready for sowing.

CROPS TO SOW

Following are the crops that can with confidence be sown in boxes prepared as advised: radish, Small-top

French Breakfast; turnip, Early Snowball; shorthorn carrot, Early Nantes; beet, Crimson Globe; onion, Spring Bunching (for salad), and mustard and cress.

An appropriate temperature for these crops is sixty degrees Fahr., but they will succeed at ten or even fifteen degrees lower though, of course, the greater the heat up to the limit I have mentioned, the more rapid the progress.

HOW TO SOW

With the exception of the mustard and cress, with which I will deal separately, broadcast the seed thinly on the surface of the compost, cover with silver or river sand, water through a fine rosed can, and place glass and brown paper over the boxes, leaving these covers in position until the seedlings show. They should then be exposed to the fullest light, and before overcrowding arises thinned (the salad onions excepted) enough to give room for proper development. Use aired water for watering, ventilate as much as the weather permits, but scrupulously avoid cold draughts, which check crops that ought to be on the move quickly.

THE SOWING PERIOD

Still leaving mustard and cress out of the account, the crops referred to above are naturally produced in the greenhouse when they cannot be grown out of doors, and when conditions in the greenhouse are favourable for their development. It is no use, for instance, sowing them between early October and the end of December. Neither the light nor the general conditions are suitable.

The effective sowing period extends from early January until the end of March, during which, if the longest possible succession is desired, radishes should be sown every ten days, and the other crops every three weeks.

71

MUSTARD AND CRESS

I refer here to the triple-leaved cress, and the black rape which is now used as a substitute for mustard, though it is known by the name of mustard. The seed leaves are larger, and there is a greater succulence about the growth. Both kinds of seed give better results if, before sowing, they are treated according to a process which resembles vernalization.

MUSTARD AND CRESS WILL GROW IN PANS, POTS OR BOXES

First steep the seed in water for twenty-four hours in a temperature of sixty degrees Fahr. On taking out the seed, dry the skins slowly in a cool room. As soon as the seed is dry, sow it very thickly on the box surface, water through a rosed can, but do not cover it with sand or soil. Place glass and brown paper over the boxes until the outline of the seed-leaves can be discerned, when full light, and perhaps one watering, are necessary to bring the crop to the cutting stage. I would indicate

72

that both mustard and cress should be cut before the normal leaves develop, or they will acquire a bitterness which makes them unpalatable.

Both salads may be produced in the greenhouse all the year round by making weekly sowings. Most people go off them during Summer, when there are plenty of outdoor salads, but these crops are specially useful because the period between seed-sowing and cutting is just under a fortnight. When other salads run short, or are likely to do so, mustard and cress can be sown to fill the breach.

AUBERGINES

In the United States edible aubergines are a very popular food crop, and are becoming more so in this country. I say edible aubergines advisedly, because the small white variety, with fruits about the size of a hen's egg, which used to be extensively cultivated as an ornamental plant, and is still by some people, is not edible. The edible kinds may be purple or white, and the fruits are of considerable size. I am sure many of my readers would like to grow aubergines.

HOW TO SOW

The seed should be sown in March or April in clean, well-drained seed-pans or boxes, in a temperature of sixty to sixty-five degrees Fahr. The seedlings come along quickly with careful watering and should, when they are nicely into rough leaf, be set separately in three-inch pots. Use a sifted compost of loam four parts, leaf mould and sand one part each, with two ounces of steamed bone meal to the pailful. Stand the plants on a light stage, and spray them lightly overhead on the mornings and afternoons of bright days. Aubergines are very susceptible to attack by red spider and thrips, and overhead spraying keeps these enemies in check.

When roots are working nicely round the sides of the soil ball, transfer the plants into six-inch pots, in which they will finish their fruits. Set them firmly in a compost of loam four parts, well-rotted manure, lime rubble and sand one part each. After the risk of night frosts is past, and the weather becomes summery, artificial heat is no longer needed, and ventilation should, except during those brief unsummer-like spells, be on a generous scale.

On most plants more fruit sets than can possibly mature. Unless growth is very vigorous, it is a good plan to reduce the fruits to four per plant. After the fruits are nicely set, feed every week with quarter strength liquid manure until ripening commences, after which feeding should cease.

Chapter XI

POTATOES, MINT AND ASPARAGUS

GROWING potatoes in the heated greenhouse is a most interesting and not unprofitable process. Perhaps the chief attraction is the earliness with which supplies can be obtained. Provided a temperature of sixty to sixty-five degrees Fahr. is maintained, the tubers are well sprouted at planting time, and quick maturing sorts such as May Queen and Ninetyfold are grown, the crop will be ready for use in about nine weeks after planting.

SPROUTING THE TUBERS

The earliest date at which it is safe to plant is mid-December. In order that the tubers may be in the right condition by that time, set them up to sprout in a light room or greenhouse having a temperature of forty-five to fifty degrees Fahr., in mid-November. Arrange them close together in clean, shallow boxes, with the round or rose end upwards, as it is from this end that the strongest sprouts proceed. No further attention is needed until planting time, when all but the strongest sprout on each tuber should be rubbed off. Better results are obtained under glass when rigorous de-sprouting is practised. Needless to say, good virile seed tubers should be used.

SPROUT POTATOES BEFORE PLANTING, BUT IN A LIGHT POSITION, OR THEY WILL BE SPINDLED, LIKE THOSE ON RIGHT OF PICTURE

I much prefer to plant potatoes under glass in nine-inch pots. Air passes through the porous sides, and there is no fear of damage from the moulds that sometimes arise when boxes of comparable depth are used. Box culture is, however, a suitable alternative when pots are not available.

HOW TO PLANT

Drain each pot with one layer of inverted crocks or potsherds, covering them with a layer of turf broken into walnut-sized pieces. Now half fill each pot with a mixture of loam three parts, leaf mould, manure and sand one part each, passing the ingredients through a half-inch sieve. Place two tubers near the centre of each pot, at four inches apart. Cover them with two inches of compost, and water through a rosed can. Obviously at this stage the pots are nothing like full. They should not be, as in the early stages it is inadvisable to give them too much rooting space.

When growth is three or four inches above the pot tops, fill the pots to within an inch of the top with the compost advised for planting. Where boxes are used, there is no need for crocks at the bottom. A two inch layer of turf answers well for drainage, provided there is a proper outlet for superfluous water through the box bottom. If there is any doubt about this, bore holes at nine inches apart. Half fill the boxes with compost to begin with, and top dress later as suggested for pots. The tubers in this case should be spaced nine inches apart.

LATER TREATMENT

It is vital to give greenhouse potatoes plenty of light, or they will develop excessive leaf growth and few or no tubers. They must be well ventilated whenever the weather is favourable, as too much atmospheric humidity is conducive to an attack of Late Blight Disease, which spreads with alarming speed in Winter.

Support each plant with a neat stake, and keep the compost pleasantly moist. Dryness prevents the tubers from swelling, while too much moisture causes them to decay. A fortnight after top dressing, stir and water into the compost around each plant a teaspoonful of a mixture of three parts superphosphate of lime, and one part each of sulphate of ammonia and sulphate of potash. This will considerably accelerate the yield and forward the maturity date. The tubers are ready for use when the haulm starts to yellow.

GREENHOUSE POTATOES GROWING IN POTS

LATE BLIGHT DISEASE

The only disease to which greenhouse potatoes are susceptible is Late Blight, the enemy which does so much damage to outdoor potatoes from July to September. The first symptoms of attack are the formation in the leaves, and sometimes the stems, of yellowish-brown blotches, which rapidly increase in size and cover with a dirty brown mould. When this phase is reached, the haulm decays speedily, and the crop must be written off as a failure.

In dealing with environmental conditions I stressed the need for avoiding excessive atmospheric humidity. It is this which gives Late Blight its chance. If the advice is followed, it is extremely unlikely that there will be an attack. If there should be, nip off and burn the affected leaves promptly, spray with Bordeaux Mixture, and the attack will be overcome.

GREEN-FLY

Potatoes in the greenhouse are subject to attack by Green-fly, which may even infest the sprouts on the seed tubers, gravely distorting them. If it does, the best way to obtain control is to dip the box containing the tubers in weak nicotine insecticide. Neither spraying nor dipping the individual tubers is effective here. Some of the flies are sure to fall off, and quickly set up new centres of attack.

Should Green-fly be found on growing plants, spraying with nicotine insecticide, or fumigation, will get rid of it. If it is decided to spray, be sure to treat the under surface of the leaves, as it is on this part of the plants that most of the insects will be found.

FORCING MINT

Mint is a great delicacy during the Winter, when anything giving a fresh herbal flavour is unobtainable from the outdoor garden. Excellent crops can be obtained in a temperature of fifty to sixty degrees Fahr. The latter temperature is preferable, as growth is more rapid and succulent.

It is not wise to lift any roots from the outdoor bed before November, by which time the crop has had some rest, and will make a good response to artificial heat. Where mint forcing is a part of the regular programme, do not force the same roots two years in succession. Let each season's forcing stock have two years in which to recover. To maintain an unbroken succession until mint is ready out of doors, plant in mid-November, mid-December and mid-January.

PRE-TREATMENT OF THE ROOTS

Take care when lifting the roots. If these are torn about with the fork, they may decay when they get into the greenhouse. A good and safe method is to lift the roots with a spade in blocks, in the same way as turf is lifted from a field. Having done so, separate the roots from the soil and wash them clean under a running tap.

A BEAUTIFUL BUNCH OF FORCED MINT

Now steep them for twenty minutes in water heated to a temperature of 118 degrees Fahr. Those who have a plunging thermometer should use it for this purpose, adding more warm water when this is necessary to maintain the requisite temperature. Where no plunging thermometer is available, keep the water pleasantly warm. The object of the treatment is to destroy the latent form of Rust Disease, which is present in so much mint. It is a successful process, so much so that I regard it as a fundamental factor in the production of mint in the greenhouse.

PLANTING EXPLAINED

Before planting, cut up the roots into one-joint pieces. The joints are plainly visible. Make each cut mid-way between each two joints. By separating the roots like this, a much better yield is secured than when they are laid out in long strings as lifted.

Boxes are very convenient receptacles in which to plant. They may be anywhere from three to six inches deep. Use a finely sifted mixture of loam three parts, leaf mould and sand one part each. After draining the boxes with an inch layer of these riddlings, fill them fairly firmly to within two inches of the top with the sifted mixture. Now spread the roots fairly thickly on the compost surface, bury them one inch deep, and water through a rosed can.

LATER TREATMENT

Few crops require less care than forcing mint. When the roots are steeped before planting, there are no disease worries, for Rust is the only possible enemy of this kind. Occasionally there is a spot of green-fly, though the essential oil in this herb is not very attractive to the pest. Should it attack, prompt fumigation will dispose of it.

Watering requires careful attention, and as growth advances a fair amount of moisture is needed. The sprigs are ready for use when about five inches long. Use scissors, and when cutting leave two leaves at the base of each sprig. From the joints of these leaves side shoots will arise, providing a most acceptable second crop.

AFTER FORCING

Many crops are useless after forcing, but this is not the case with mint. It is true that having given one crop, no more sprigs should be taken in that particular season, but if the roots are re-planted in the garden, they will give an abundant crop the next year, and in the season following will, if required, be ready for forcing again. An ideal way of re-planting is to knock one end out of each box and slide the contents carefully into a suitable hole made in well-manured soil. This is far better than shaking out the roots and re-planting them separately.

FORCING ASPARAGUS

Forced asparagus is ranked as an epicure's dish, and no wonder. It is within everybody's reach, but at the outset I would make it clear that nobody should lift established roots for forcing from an outdoor bed. That would mean the sacrifice of an excellent garden feature for a temporary pleasure, as asparagus roots after forcing are of no further use. Fortunately, nurserymen make a practice of offering three-year-old roots for forcing at very reasonable prices. Secure some of these.

THE PLANTING ENVIRONMENT

Asparagus may be planted in boxes, or in a bed on the greenhouse stage. Personally, I prefer the latter method, as it offers a better chance of keeping the soil evenly moist, and this is a most important factor. Good results, however, are obtained in boxes, which should be at least twelve inches deep.

Where the stage bed can be arranged, spread on the stage a four-inch layer of strawy manure or straw. Cover this with four inches of sifted soil, old potting soil being quite suitable. Spread on the soil an inch layer of sand, to ensure that free porosity which asparagus loves. The crop, as indicated, likes moisture, but this must not linger around the roots. Space the latter four inches apart, cover them with four inches of soil, and water through a rosed can. Prepare and plant boxes on similar lines.

MANAGEMENT OF THE CROP

From beginning to end maintain a temperature of sixty to sixty-five degrees Fahr., and ensure a fair amount of light. After growth starts, spray the beds daily with aired water, and feed weekly with agricultural salt solution (one ounce in a gallon of water, and one gallon per square yard per dose). Asparagus is a crop of maritime origin, and there is no fertilizer like salt for bringing the best out of forcing crowns.

It may be that some of the spears or shoots will have difficulty in pushing through. Instead of growing erect, as they should, they curve. This bent finger, as it is called, is usually induced by some hard object such as a bit of turf or a pebble. If the obstruction is removed promptly, the shoot will take its normal shape. Very little ventilation is desirable. The atmosphere must not be allowed to become too dry, nor yet too moist. Every gardener knows that there is a happy medium between these two extremes, and that he can maintain it by judicious ventilation. The spears, which are ready for cutting when they are seven or eight inches long, should be severed cleanly well beneath the bed surface.

ASPARAGUS ENEMIES

No disease attacks forcing asparagus if the crowns are sound when put in. If there is Crown Rot in any of them, there will be no growth from the affected. When it is seen that there is going to be no growth, lift and burn the diseased roots, for Crown Rot has a habit of spreading in the soil.

The ubiquitous Green-fly may assail the developing spears. Fumigation quickly exterminates it. Wood-lice are occasionally troublesome. They can be cleared out by sprinkling on the bed a mixture of equal parts dried blood and pyrethrum powder. The latter, which is non-poisonous to human beings, is fatal to the wood-lice, which pick it up when they come after the, to them, irresistible dried blood. Nor must it be forgotten that rats and mice are just as fond of asparagus as we are. It may be essential to trap or poison these rodents.

Chapter XII

RHUBARB, SEAKALE, CHICORY, TURNIP TOPS AND POTATOES

GOOD use can be made of the heated greenhouse as a forcing environment, and rhubarb is prominent amongst the crops that can be raised there. By planting in November, December and January it is possible to gather beautiful forced rhubarb from Christmas until outdoor supplies are ready.

SELECTING THE FORCING STOCK

The varieties Prince Albert and Champagne, being early sorts in the outdoor garden, are good ones to choose for the first planting in the greenhouse. Earliness is their characteristic wherever they are grown. For the two last plantings Victoria, Linnæus and Dawe's Champion are of outstanding value, though it should be said that where only one variety is available, it can be used for the three plantings. If a late variety is planted early, it will take it a little longer to reach maturity. That is the only disadvantage.

Roots under three years old should not be forced. There is not sufficient reserve material in the crowns to produce a worth-while crop. Nor is it advisable to force roots two years in succession. After forcing, they should be given two seasons in which to recuperate. Having cleared up the matter of age of crown and periodicity of forcing, I would stress the necessity for selecting for forcing bold and substantial crowns. Success is sure to attend the forcing of them if the right principles are followed. The crowns, by the way, are the finger-like processes at the top of the roots.

EXPOSING THE ROOTS

Before rhubarb roots are planted in the forcing environment, they should be exposed to the elements for a fortnight to retard them. To do this make a trench round each root, push the spade blade beneath it, heave upwards, turn the roots upside down, and let them receive the full blast of the weather—frost, snow, rain, hail or wind.

This operation appears somewhat vicious, and doubtless is, for it reduces the growth activity in the crowns to the barest minimum consistent with the maintenance of life itself. That is just what is wanted by the forcer of rhubarb, for when he plants his roots in heat, they respond markedly to the genial conditions, and endeavour to make up, as it were, for what was lost by the exposure. So pivotal is this prior lifting that I go so far as to say that good rhubarb cannot be forced without it.

HOW TO PLANT THE ROOTS

At the end of the exposure period plant the roots in the position they are to occupy until the crop has been gathered. Essentials to success are absolute darkness and some artificial heat. The ideal temperature is fifty-five to sixty degrees Fahr., and where possible the thermometer should be maintained at this level, in the interests of the greatest success. Most gardeners, how- ever, cannot devote a greenhouse altogether to the forcing of rhubarb. It must provide shelter for subjects of varying requirements. For that reason it is often essential to effect a compromise.

FORCED RHUBARB GROWING FREELY

In this connection it should be said that rhubarb will force well in any temperature from forty to sixty-five degrees Fahr. The lower the temperature the slower, of course, will be the growth, but no attempt should be made to secure rhubarb earlier by lifting before the third week in October. Until that period the crop has not had sufficient rest, and in consequence forces badly, if at all.

Usually the most convenient position is beneath the greenhouse stage, the front of which is draped to exclude the light. If the hot water pipes run beneath the stage, a board should be interposed between these pipes and the rhubarb bed, to prevent undue drying out.

Deep boxes covered with sacks, or large pots covered with inverted pots of even size, may also be used, while good batches of rhubarb can be forced on the stage provided light is excluded. Set the roots three to four inches apart on a four-inch layer of ordinary garden soil, packing similar soil between them until only the crowns or tops are exposed. This soil must be pressed firmly, for in a spongy or uneven bed it is impossible to get the even moisture conditions that forced rhubarb requires.

THE MANAGEMENT OF THE CROP

Immediately after planting, soak the bed with clear water, and until the crop is finished water whenever the soil shows signs of drying. If forcing rhubarb is ever permitted to dry out, the stems will bend over and never straighten again. Every morning spray the surface of the bed with clear, aired water, to promote the most vigorous growth.

The first indication of any change is the swelling of the crowns, which also become quite pink. After this swelling has reached its maximum, the stems burst through a veil stretched tightly over the crowns. When they do this, it can be considered that the crop is safely on its way. Sometimes, however, the veil remains tight, and will not burst at the behest of the stems pressing from the under-surface. When it is observed that there is a growth lock of this kind, slit the reluctant veil with a safety-razor blade, and all will be well. If no action is taken, the stems will rot and that particular crown become a liability.

When the stems are three inches long, feed the bed with quarter strength liquid manure (one gallon per square yard). This primarily nitrogeneous fertilizer encourages a speedy, succulent and tasty growth.

GATHERING RHUBARB AND AFTERWARDS

The stems are ready to gather when they are twelve to eighteen inches long, according to variety and the thickness of the stems themselves. When gathering grip each stem firmly at the base, and twist and pull simultaneously. By adopting this method the stem right to its base is able to leave the socket cleanly, and there is no damage to the crowns. Should the stem be pulled only, that is, without the twist, the short stub that is inevitably left in the socket will decay and interfere with subsequent production.

When all the crop has been collected, transfer the roots straight away to an outdoor bed of cinders or sand, and heel them in four inches deep until early March, when they should be planted three feet apart in deeply dug, rich soil. At planting time just bury the crowns.

BACTERIAL DISEASE

Bacterial Disease is the only enemy which the forcer of rhubarb need consider. It is, however, a formidable enemy. The crowns and roots are attacked by putrefactive bacteria, which induce them to decay rapidly. In the great rhubarb districts of the country, notably the one near Leeds, this disease at one time threatened the very existence of the industry. It was by rigid selection and burning the infected roots that Bacterial Disease was held in leash. If the crop and the bacteria had been left to fight it out, the position to-day might have been very serious indeed.

I do hope, on account of the persistent character of bacterial trouble, that my readers will keep a careful watch for it, and if they observe that in the forcing bed a crown or crowns are sinking, and that on further investigation decay is proceeding, they will dig up that root and burn it. Bacterial Disease is there, and there is no remedy for it but cremation.

The search should extend beyond the forcing bed. From time to time rhubarb needs dividing, and when it has been split up, the beginnings of Bacterial Disease, where present, can be traced. There will be dark streaky marks in the internal tissues of the crowns. Even though at the moment there seem to be cropping potentialities, such plants should be destroyed. The incubus is on them, and will gradually become heavier and heavier until perhaps the garden may for the time being have ceased to become a rhubarb-growing centre.

FORCING SEAKALE

Seakale has in the past, to a large extent, been regarded as a rich man's dish. I do not make that observation with any desire to reflect on either rich men or poor men. I merely record the fact. Now why seakale should not have found its way into the home of everyone who has a heated greenhouse I cannot tell, for in Winter and early Spring seakale makes a most appetizing dish. To maintain a long succession, plantings should be made in early December, early January and early February, respectively.

The crop is, of course, grown in the outdoor garden, and with its cultivation there we are not concerned in this book. The roots are lifted in early October, the side roots removed, and the tap roots stored in sand in a frost-proof place, to be withdrawn as required. Those who have no seakale in their garden, and who do not feel like allocating space to the crop, can buy from nurserymen roots specially grown for forcing. The price is about thirty shillings per hundred, and when one considers the volume of choice produce that can be raised from this number of roots, the price is most reasonable.

PLANTING SEAKALE

Seakale requires a similar environment to that prescribed for rhubarb, with the exception that the temperature should not fall below forty-five degrees Fahr., otherwise the stems will be short and poor. Whether the beneath-stage border, pot or box method is followed, the roots should be set five inches apart, leaving the top inch

FORCED SEAKALE—A TASTY WINTER VEGETABLE

exposed. Take care when planting not to damage the roots, as bruising is often followed by decay.

ATTENTIONS TO THE GROWING CROP

While seakale soil should never be allowed really to dry out, the crop does not require quite as much water as rhubarb. Just keep the bed pleasantly moist, and when the stems are about two inches long feed with sulphate of ammonia solution (one ounce to the gallon of water), and growth will go speedily forward with all that beautiful succulence possessed by well forced seakale.

The crop is ready for cutting when the stems are about ten inches long, and when cutting it slice off about half an inch of the crowns. The stems will then remain in good condition if no more than a reasonable period elapses before they are prepared for the table. After forcing, the roots are of no further use, and should be thrown away.

BLACK ROT DISEASE

Seakale roots are liable to be attacked by the Black Rot Disease, which has many hosts, including delphiniums, lupins, peas, beans and potatoes. It will be seen, therefore, that in the average garden there is no lack of possible infective material. The symptoms are the development of black decay lesions in the crowns or root tops. As it is from these points that growth proceeds, the evil potentialities of Black Rot can be surmised. If nothing is done, infected roots will be ruined, and one wood-louse crawling over a decay lesion can carry sufficient infection to spoil an entire batch. Happily Black Rot can easily be overcome by cutting off the affected parts and burning them, and dusting the exposed surface with flowers of sulphur.

FORCING CHICORY

This is another crop that ought to be more universally forced. Many people are acquainted with it, as before the war they bought Belgian chicory in the shops. It made a greatly appreciated addition to the salad selection in Winter. Chicory roots are easily produced in the garden from seed sown in April or May. In October these roots are lifted and stored in sand in a frost-proof environment until they are required.

Forcing commences in early November, and at three-weekly intervals relays of roots are planted. Before planting, cut off the bottom one-third of each root, dipping the cut end in dry soil to prevent bleeding. This somewhat strange procedure is adopted for two reasons. Often chicory roots have such long tails that it is well-nigh impossible to plant them conveniently in the greenhouse as they are. Secondly, there is no doubt that cutting retards, as exposure does in the case of rhubarb, thus ensuring a quicker and fuller yield.

HOW TO PLANT CHICORY

I need not dwell long on this matter, so far as one aspect of it goes, for chicory can successfully be planted in exactly the same way as advocated for seakale. There is another method, too, and it promotes even greater succulence. The roots are spaced five inches apart in a bed of ordinary garden soil beneath the greenhouse stage, or in deep boxes, and are covered with ten inches of soil or leaf mould. When growth starts it naturally pushes its way to the light, prompted by negative geotropism, and in endeavouring to make this journey quickly, develops a succulence that must be seen to be believed.

Forcing chicory in this way certainly involves a little more work, but I strongly recommend it to those who have the time. Cut the heads with an inch of crown when they are eight to ten inches long. If the supply is likely to run short, each batch of roots will produce a second crop. On the top of the cut roots other growth crowns form, and though the second cutting is not quite as good as the first, it more than justifies the space it takes and the labour it involves. After the first or second forcing, as the case may be, the roots are of no further horticultural value, though if dried and ground they make quite a good substitute for coffee.

TURNIP TOPS

Most people grow true turnips or Swedish turnips, but only a limited number make use of the rejected crowns for forcing. When the housewife is preparing turnips or swedes for the table, she cuts off about an inch at the top, because this part is tough and indigestible. It is the part, however, in which the latent growth buds reside, and this growth can be forced out of them by just heeling the tops in a box of leaf mould, or soil containing plenty of leaf mould, keeping the soil moist and the box dark. The usual method is to stand the box under the greenhouse stage. In course of time plenty of blanched stems and rudimentary leaves develop. These, when cut and cooked as a second vegetable, make a dish with a pronounced seakale flavour.

POTATOES

In Chapter XI, page 74. I dealt with one method of growing potatoes in the heated greenhouse. Here is an alternative method which properly belongs to this chapter. It consists in selecting a number of large ware potatoes, and planting them four inches apart and three inches deep in a box of sifted leaf mould. Stand the box in any convenient part of the greenhouse, keep the leaf mould moist, and in due course, usually about eight weeks, the potatoes planted will have more or less disappeared, and their place be taken by a large number of small tubers possessing the new potato flavour. The weight lifted will be the weight planted, plus the water absorbed. The method may be more novel than remunerative ; nevertheless, it is very nice to taste new potatoes in Winter. Why not raise some for next Christmas dinner?

CLEANLINESS ESSENTIAL

It is imperative that the environment in which all crops are forced shall be as clean as it can be made. Before planting, dispose of all litter, and wash down with water or limewash. In the absence of such a precaution wood-lice, crickets and millipedes may cause a good deal of trouble.

Guard against fluctuations of temperature, as checks in growth impair the succulence of the crop. When lifting mats or other covers that exclude light, see that they are properly replaced. A chink of light reaching the forcing bed is enough to rob the crop concerned of its blanch, and if that goes, the forcing effort is less successful than it might have been.

Chapter XIII

RAISING VEGETABLE SEEDLINGS

THE heated greenhouse presents an ideal environment for the raising of seedlings that ultimately find their way into the open garden. In some cases, as in that of outdoor tomatoes, the season is not long enough to allow for sowing entirely out of doors. Some protection must be given in the early stages. In some cases, such as that of early Summer cauliflowers, under-glass protection for a few weeks makes it possible for the gardener to cut the crop earlier.

PREPARATION OF THE SEED BOXES

Ideal seed boxes are two feet long, one foot wide, and two and a half inches deep. Before use they ought, in the interests of hygiene, to be brushed well out, and steeped in boiling water or dipped in a sterilizing fluid prepared in accordance with the manufacturer's instructions. The compost should be sterilized too, thus eliminating the risk of trouble from the many microscopic foes that can do such irreparable harm in a seed box. I have already dealt with compost sterilization in Chapter II, page 21. It would be superfluous to cover the ground again.

A good general compost in which to raise vegetable seedlings is loam three parts, leaf mould and sand one part each, with an ounce of superphosphate of lime to the pailful. Pass the two first-named ingredients through a half-inch sieve, to ensure an even texture, and make certain of thorough mixing by turning over the heap three or four times.

Use a three-quarters of an inch layer of the rough riddlings for draining the boxes, afterwards filling them up fairly firmly with compost to within half an inch of the top. Now level the latter with a flat board, and all is ready for sowing.

HOW TO SOW THE SEED

Tomato, leek and onion seed should be spaced an inch apart, other kinds distributed very thinly out of a hole in the corner of the seed packet, or from a piece of white paper creased down the middle. The latter is an excellent device for those who are not too sure about the steadiness of their hand. It enables them to control the distribution perfectly.

Having sown the seed, just cover it with silver or river sand, or compost passed through a quarter of an inch sieve. Now comes watering through a fine rosed can, using aired water. As soon as the boxes have drained, place glass and brown paper over them with the object of maintaining stable conditions during the germinating period. It is just as well to place a label or a pebble between the top of each box and the glass covering it, as a safeguard against over-wetness. Unless this is done, the volume of water that collects on the glass will ultimately drop on to the compost and make it so wet that the seed affected by the drip may rot.

During the germinating period stand the boxes in a draught-free corner of the house, or in the propagating frame, removing the covers as soon as growth shows. From then onwards sufficient light is necessary to keep growth sturdy, remembering that during the first few days it may be essential to shade slightly. Now I deal with the actual vegetables to be raised.

THE CABBAGE FAMILY

Early February is a good time to sow the following reliable members of the cabbage family : Brussels sprout, The Favourite ; cauliflower, May Queen ; cabbage, Primo. The first-named goes out into the garden in mid-May, the cabbages and cauliflowers in late April. When the seedlings are big enough to handle, transplant them into other boxes at two inches apart, selecting sturdy specimens. The markedly vigorous are invariably hybrids, while the markedly weak are afflicted with a constitutional defect which cannot be eliminated. The vital factor with these vegetables is to transplant before there is over-crowding, which owing to the rapidity of growth soon occurs.

ONIONS

Sow in early January for planting out in late April. Premier and Big Ben are splendid sorts. There are two ways of treating the seedlings. One is to set them separately in thumb pots. This method, by avoiding root disturbance at the final planting time, is much favoured by exhibitors, who must, if they are to secure the prizes, see that their plants receive no check. The alternative is to plant at two inches apart in boxes, and in both cases care must be taken just to bury the roots only. Deeply planted onions invariably develop thick neck.

EARLY LEEKS

Splendid early leeks for mid-May planting can be raised in the greenhouse from a mid-February sowing. Treat the seedlings precisely as advised for onions, and choose a proven sort such as Musselburgh or White Column.

ONION SEEDLINGS RAISED IN THE GREENHOUSE

TOMATOES

Tomatoes for planting out in early June should be sown the second or third week in March. Varieties that have given outstanding returns in the past few years are Harbinger, Sensation, and Pride of the Garden. Make a firm resolve to secure strong plants in four and a half inch pots by the time mentioned. The season is short for outdoor tomatoes, and it is, therefore, a great help to begin with good material.

To this end transplant the seedlings at two inches apart into boxes as soon as they are big enough to handle, moving them as required into two and a half and four and a half inch pots respectively.

CELERY, CELERIAC AND PARSLEY

Sow the celery Vhite Plume and celeriac Giant Prague in mid-February for planting out at the end of May, and the parsley Myatt's Garnishing in mid-February for planting out in mid-April. In all cases, unless the seed has already been treated by the seedsman, sterilize it for three hours in commercial formalin solution, as a safeguard against Leaf Blight Disease. Prepare the solution by stirring a medicinal drachm of commercial formalin into two and a half pints of water. Empty the seed into the solution, stir it every half hour, and on taking it out dry it slowly. The seedlings when they are big enough to move, should be transplanted at two inches apart into boxes.

CUCUMBERS AND VEGETABLE MARROWS

The end of March is an appropriate period at which to sow the vegetable marrow Long Green or Long Cream, and the ridge cucumber Stockwood Prize or Wither's Prize Ridge, separately in three and a half inch pots for transplanting to the final quarters in early June. Press each seed in edgeways with the finger-tip one quarter of an inch to half an inch deep, to make sure of a perfectly formed seedling. Water the plants carefully without splashing the stems, and they will develop into sturdy specimens.

RUNNER AND FRENCH BEANS

Earlier crops of runner and French beans can be secured by sowing at the end of March, and planting out in late May. Set the seed three inches apart in boxes, and just bury it. Do not water until the seedlings show, and for a time afterwards water cautiously. Too much water in these early days stunts the growth that one is wishing to encourage. After the plants get well into rough leaf they will, of course, take more generous supplies.

MISCELLANEOUS CROPS

An early lettuce, such as Continuity, sage, thyme, balm, marjoram, fennel, rue, Good King Henry, and even spinach, are other examples of crops that can be forwarded under glass for planting out. Sow them in boxes in early February, prick out the seedlings into other boxes when they are big enough to handle, and they will be ready for their permanent places about the middle of April.

HARDENING OFF IN THE COLD FRAME

HARDENING OFF

It follows that these vegetables, having been raised in an environment which protects them from every unkindly influence, develop a succulent and tender growth. Temporarily they are exotics. There is no doubt about that. It would, in consequence, be fatal to transfer them straight from the greenhouse to an open air life. There must be an intermediate phase, and this is technically known as hardening off.

The process must be gradual, and should start about three weeks before the final planting. Transfer the boxes to a cold frame, choosing a genial day, or affording some protection on the journey. During the first three days keep the frame closed, unless the sun is so powerful that a little air must be given to prevent scorch. On the second three days admit three or four inches of air to each light. From the end of the sixth day ventilate progressively on a more generous scale until, during the first three days of the last week, the lights can be removed altogether, but replaced at night. On the last three days give no protection at all. This treatment ensures easy transition from the greenhouse to the garden.

I do not wish my readers to imagine that the programme is as unalterable as the laws of the Medes and Persians. It can apply precisely as given if the weather is normal. Should there be a sudden setback, however, keep the lights closed or nearly so until it passes. All gardeners should remember that absolute inflexibility is a rule that cannot and should not be observed by them.

SECTION II

Chapter XIV

THE UNHEATED GREENHOUSE

MORE people than ever are now making use of the unheated greenhouse, owing to the difficulty of obtaining fuel and the cost of such supplies as are available. I am not going to pretend that a greenhouse without artificial heat is as good a crop-raising unit as one in which the temperature can be fixed at any desired level by means of hot water circulating in the pipes. There are limitations regarding the type of crop that can be grown, and in various ways procedure must be altered. It will be our business to examine this part of the programme as we proceed. Meanwhile, I wish to make it clear that if the limitations are recognized, and regard is paid to the peculiar conditions in an unheated house, excellent results can be obtained therein.

ON VENTILATING

Ventilation should be carefully studied. In Spring, Autumn and Winter, for instance, there are many days on which the sun attains sufficient power to create warm and genial conditions within the house. The ventilators must, of course, be opened when the sun is out, unless there is a keen frost which cancels its heat, but they should be closed early enough in the afternoon to husband some of that valuable natural heat which, except in the very coldest periods, will keep the thermometer well above freezing point during the night.

Artificial heat dries up atmospheric moisture. In the absence of it the atmosphere will become overcharged unless there is judicious ventilation. The air will become clammy and unhealthy, and the crops will show a marked susceptibility to the diseases that attack them. In damp periods, therefore, do see that the ventilators are opened sufficiently to avoid clamminess, and keep the air moving.

Windy days present their problems. A brisk wind, for instance, from a cold quarter will, if it blows directly into a house, impose a severe check on growth. That is why, on such days, the ventilators should always be opened on the leeward side. It is a great advantage to have ventilators in the sides of the house for use on days like these. Cold winds do not find them quite so easily as they find ventilators fixed on the roof.

WATERING

Watering is one of the first essentials of plant life, therefore crops in unheated houses must receive of this what is essential for them. But caution must be used. Thus, from mid-September until mid-May plants that require water should receive it in the morning, so that the drainings and any moisture that is not actually absorbed by the soil can dry up before night. Morning watering is also advisable for the same reason during cool, dull periods in Summer, but in warm spells water in the early evening.

In Winter, crops in unheated houses, lettuce excepted, must be kept markedly on the dry side. Actually, what the gardener terms a dry soil contains quite a good volume of water in association with the soil particles. The roots can obtain from this what is required to keep them alive and healthy, and nothing more is expected during the periods I have described.

Do not when watering, except during warm, bright periods, water the house as well as the plants. Avoid splashing between pots and boxes, on stages and paths. Just pour the water into the pots or boxes, thus making a marked contribution to atmospheric health. In bright and sunny times, of course water, on the paths and stages is health-giving, as it prevents the aridity which is not helpful to growth, and which is conducive to infestations of pests.

The question of stage breeze can conveniently be considered here. This material, whether it be sifted cinders, shingle, or small coke itself, absorbs a great deal of moisture, which depresses the temperature and acts as a harbour for slugs, which can be something of a nuisance in the unheated house in Winter. I suggest that this material should be removed at the end of September and replaced at the end of March. A Winter's exposure to the elements will do it all the good in the world.

WINTRY SPELLS

Wintry spells, by which I mean very severe frosts and heavy and prolonged snowstorms, are a source of anxiety to the owner of the unheated house, but if the right programme is pursued very little, if any, damage will be done. Where the house is fitted with lath blinds, they are a great blessing, because they can be run down at night when it looks as if the temperature would fall below freezing point.

These lath blinds are rather expensive and difficult to secure just now. Useful alternatives are found in tiffany, scrim, old coco-matting, sacks opened out and sewn together, and so on. If whatever is used is attached to a lath top and bottom, it can with little difficulty be rolled out over a house of average size, excluding frost.

If external protection is difficult or impossible, a similar result can be obtained inside the house by standing the plants close together and covering them with newspapers or scrim or, alternatively, by standing them under the stage and fixing some kind of protection round the outside. The plants are thus placed in a closed compartment, in which it will take a very keen frost to reach them.

As hard frost often accompanies snow, similar protective measures may be called for. It is vital that I should indicate what should be done with the snow on the glass. This is in itself a protection, and no effort should be made to move it for a week. At the end of that period, however, another factor, namely, lack of light, intervenes. The crops will spindle, become super-succulent and out of character, unless the snow is swept off the glass. It becomes a duty to remove a protective influence in order to admit another influence of even greater significance.

IF CROPS ARE FROSTED

Robert Burns told us that " the best laid schemes of mice and men gang aft a-gley." Sometimes the owner of the unheated greenhouse, for example, is caught napping. An unexpected frost occurs, and he finds that the crops on which he had set great store are covered with rime. Now in the act of freezing it is seldom that any real damage is done. A few cells are ruptured, but it is not beyond the power of the plants to repair them. The sap leaves the majority of cells without harming them, and is deposited as crystals on the cell walls. If those crystals can be melted slowly, the cells have a chance of re-absorbing their own sap, in which case the normal course of life and growth will be resumed.

Should there be a rapid thaw, the melted crystals will cause chaotic flooding and death. It follows on this account that where the crops are frosted, the grower should do his best to induce a slow thaw. This can be accomplished by spraying the plants with ice-cold water, and keeping them in the dark until their rimed and some-what drooping leaves again become normal. One thing must be avoided, that of allowing a rapid thaw, which frequently follows a night of severe frost. If that occurs, the plants will be black, soppy and dead.

These are all the special points that need be mentioned in connection with the management of the unheated house. It will be seen that they do not involve a great deal of labour or skill, and having regard to the excellent results that are possible, the extra effort is well worth while.

Chapter XV

CROPS IN THE UNHEATED GREENHOUSE

ALL the crops that I recommended for the heated greenhouse can be produced satisfactorily in the unheated structure. Naturally, there are modifications of practice which I shall point out in the appropriate place, but I would indicate that the general principles enunciated in former chapters apply here. It would, therefore, be superfluous for me to repeat them. To give an example which makes clear the point I desire to impress. Tomatoes grown in the unheated greenhouse are subject to attack by the same pests and diseases as those in the heated house, and similar preventions or remedies are efficacious. They should be grown in sterilized compost, be regularly trimmed and tied, watered and fed. In short, it is just the different temperature that calls in some respects for a different approach to the cultural problem. And so the position applies to every crop. I will now proceed to deal with the special technique for an unheated house.

TOMATOES

In the South and Midlands the end of April is an appropriate time to plant tomatoes in an unheated house. North of the Trent mid-May is a safe period. Having regard to the fact that planting is later than in a heated structure, and owing to the fact that there may be temporary checks, it is open to serious question whether the owner of an unheated greenhouse should attempt to raise his own seedlings. He cannot sow before mid-March in any part of the country, and even then special means must be employed. The seedlings should be inside a glass-covered box, and there is much to be said for standing the box on a vessel which is filled with hot water two or three times a day, to give bottom heat. Is that programme worth while ?

I suggest that it is not, and that a better course would be to order from the nurseryman plants in three inch pots, to be delivered at a specified time. Do ask for these some weeks before they are required, to give the nurseryman a fair chance to fulfil his part of the contract. The perilous times are those in which there are violent changes. There are a few warm days, followed by a few cold ones. Or after a drought, several days of muggy, wet weather set in. Seeing that there is no heat in the house with which to equalize conditions, it is only natural that the crop should make an adverse reaction. In cold weather the foliage turns blue, in damp conditions there is a greatly increased liability to Cladosporium and Stem Rot Diseases.

Happily, by using careful judgment, these difficulties can be overcome. During cold periods, for example, watering should be reduced to the very minimum, and the ventilators opened only sufficiently to avoid atmospheric clamminess. Minimum watering is an obvious necessity in wet times, but during these the ventilators should be opened as widely as possible, with a view to preventing absolute humidity, in which an outbreak of the diseases I have mentioned is a veritable certainty.

FEEDING AND VARIETIES

Tomatoes in the unheated house need nitrogen just as much as do those assisted by artificial heat, but the supply should be most carefully regulated. Thus I suggest that no liquid manure, soluble dried blood, or other form of nitrogen should be applied during the sultry periods, or the growth will be made much too succulent and prone to attack by Cladosporium. Keep it firm and resistant by giving each plant every five days a teaspoonful of a mixture of three parts superphosphate of lime and two parts sulphate or muriate of potash.

In raising or ordering varieties, ask for those which, while being good croppers, are known to be tolerant of atmospheric and temperature changes. In this category are Sunrise, Potentate, Ailsa Craig and Market King.

MELONS

The real hot-house melon will not succeed in an unheated greenhouse. Even if it is possible to induce the fruits to set, swell and ripen, the flavour will be indifferent. In this category are Emerald Gem, Montreal, Royal Sovereign, Superlative and King George. Ban them altogether, concentrating on Munro's Little Heath or Hero of Lockinge. Both are net melons, the former being scarlet-fleshed, the latter white-fleshed. The flavour of both is superb.

It is recognized that the earlier the fruits are ripened the choicer the flavour, hence the seed should be sown as soon as it is safe to do so. This will be the first week in May in the South and Midlands, the second week North of the Trent. Plunge the pots to the rim in fibre or leaf mould previously warmed in an oven or similar place, to induce that rapid germination which contributes so much to vigour in a melon plant. Empty the leaf mould or fibre into a glass-covered box as a further aid.

The plants will do very well set out as advised in Chapter VI, but I know that everybody wishes to give this fruit the best possible chance. That can be done by setting the mounds or borders on a nine-inch layer of fermenting manure, or in the case of pots or boxes surrounding these receptacles with a six-inch layer of similar material. A little heat round or beneath the roots is greatly appreciated.

In a heated house one can be very free with the syringe on melons. They like this. It creates a good Turkish bath-like, growing atmosphere. There are many occasions during Summer when plants in an unheated house can be treated similarly. There are other occasions, namely, when the outside atmosphere is heavy with moisture, on which it would be most unwise to syringe under glass. The air is already humid enough. So desist on these occasions.

And at all times be very watchful for Mildew, which spreads rapidly. Immediately it appears, destroy the fungus responsible by dusting with flowers of sulphur or green sulphur powder. If these precautions are observed, a splendid crop of beautifully flavoured fruit will be raised.

CUCUMBERS, MARROWS AND SQUASHES

The varieties of vegetable marrow and squash which I advised for the heated greenhouse do equally well in the absence of artificial heat, but I specially praise the cucumber Conqueror for such conditions. It crops amazingly. Appropriate sowing times for the South are the last week in April, for the North the first week in May. One sowing of vegetable marrows and squashes will be sufficient, but if a second batch of cucumbers is desired, this may be inserted the last week in June.

Beyond carefully adjusting the ventilation in accordance with the weather, there are no special precautions to observe.

FRENCH BEANS

The unheated greenhouse can with advantage be used to raise an early crop of French beans, and some remarkably fine pods can be produced therein. Lightning is a notably good sort. If sown the third week in April in the South, and the last week of that month in the Midlands and North, the crop will be ready for gathering in June, or at the latest early July.

A point that calls for careful notice is that of a May frost sufficiently severe to find its way into the house. Of course, the risk of this is greatly minimized if the ventilators are closed early enough to husband some natural heat, but even this may not be sufficient if the thermometer falls to twenty degrees Fahr. or thereabouts, as it does occasionally in this very fickle month. Luckily the gardener is usually warned by a bright sky and the rapid descent of the temperature about sunset. When such a warning is given, prudence demands that the French beans should be covered with newspaper or some light fabric.

Inevitable temperature changes which are outside the danger zone sometimes induce semi-chlorosis or pale-leaf. Instead of being that rich green which betokens robust health, the plants assume that sickly green which causes them to set their pods badly, and drop some of those which they have set. Should such a crop-reducing phenomenon occur, restore the plants to normality by watering them with sulphate of iron solution (one quarter of an ounce in two gallons of water), giving just as much as would be given if they were being watered ordinarily.

PEAS

The unheated greenhouse is a first class environment for the production of early peas. Sowings may be made in January, February or March, but I would prefer to put the seed in in November, choosing a hardy, round-seeded variety such as the eighteen inch tall Eclipse, or the two feet tall Superb.

Where tomatoes are grown in permanent borders, the seed may be sown in them in the same way as it is sown in the open garden. After the tomatoes are cleared, and the house is washed down, fork the borders a foot deep, break down the lumps tread moderately, and rake the surface even. Do not incorporate any stable manure or compost. This is quite unnecessary, as the tomatoes have left behind them a residue of this kind of food adequate to see the crop through. Do, however, rake in a two ounce per square yard dressing of steamed bone flour, which will help materially at pod-filling time.

Make the drills six inches wide, one and a half inches deep, and space them two feet apart. As mice frequently find their way into the greenhouse in Winter, protect the seed from them by steeping it in paraffin for three minutes and rolling it in red lead immediately before sowing. Space the seed three inches apart. As the seedlings develop, support them with tree branches or stakes and string, and always keep the soil slightly on the dry side. As soon as flowering finishes, remove the growing points to concentrate food in the developing pods, ventilate as generously as the weather permits, and a very fine crop will result.

PEAS GROWING IN THE UNHEATED GREENHOUSE

PEAS IN BOXES AND POTS

Where there is no permanent border in the greenhouse, the alternative method of growing peas in four-inch deep boxes or six-inch pots is eminently successful. A little more water is needed here, as the roots are more confined and cannot search for moisture as they can in an open border. Do not, however, allow the soil to become too moist, or the plants will yellow and go off with Foot Rot. Space the seed three inches apart, and set it an inch deep in November, as advised for borders.

BROAD BEANS

Broad beans, like peas, are leguminous crops, and their requirements in an unheated greenhouse are almost exactly similar to those of peas. The only difference is that of seed spacing. Where the permanent border method is followed, set two rows of seed alternately at six inches apart in each drill, and where pots or boxes are used, allow five inches between the seeds. The varieties Seville Giant Longpod and Early Mazagan are reliable in every respect.

LETTUCE

I consider that the varieties Cheshunt Early Ball and Loos Tennis Ball are the two leading lettuces for the unheated house. Their great qualifications are that they will form hearts when the temperature is just above freezing point, and that they are very resistant to Mildew. It is extremely doubtful whether pre-Christmas sowings are of much use. I have tried sowing in September and October, and the crops made satisfactory progress until the November and December fogs came along, when they lost ground heavily. They did not actually die, but plants from early January sowings were ready to cut just as soon, and on the whole were better.

In an evenly mild and comparatively fog-free Winter these early sowings would be profitable, and would yield lettuce for cutting quite early in the New Year. But such seasons are so rare that I ask my readers whether it is not better to omit these sowings and start in early January, when the days are getting lighter and there is a real growth urge. Succession sowings may be made in early February and early March.

NOTE THESE POINTS

On the foundation principles of greenhouse lettuce growing I need not enlarge, as these were dealt with fully in Chapter IV. Two or three matters, however, must be observed. One is the tendency for a green scum to form on the soil or compost surface before the roots become really active. If that is allowed to remain, the degree of sourness will be such that root action never will be satisfactory. Scrape off this scum should it appear, and sprinkle a little lime on the soil as a deterrent to further souring.

There may be times when the temperature in the house will be below freezing point. Root action will then cease, or nearly so. Important as is moisture to lettuce, none should be given under these conditions. Wait until the crop again has a chance to grow. Though the varieties concerned are resistant to Mildew, it does not follow that they never contract it. On the contrary, during persistent bad weather spells the disease gains an entrance. As soon as the purplish-white mould is seen on the leaves, dust with green sulphur powder to free the crop from this enemy.

POTATOES

Potatoes will bear three or four degrees of frost without showing any sign of injury. It is authoritatively stated that if protective measures are taken, such as covering with inverted pots or light fabric, twelve degrees can be excluded. As we do not have frost as keen as this in average years after the end of the first week in March, potatoes may be planted in the unheated greenhouse at that period. They will be ready for lifting by the end of May if the principles suggested in Chapter XI are followed.

MINT

The forcing of this crop proceeds on similar lines to those described in Chapter XII. The plantings may be at the same time also. Of course, the progress of the growth will be slower, but that is all the difference there will be. The quality of the produce will be quite as satisfactory.

FORCED ROOTS

In this category are asparagus, rhubarb, seakale and chicory. As some heat is necessary to force growth out of these roots, it follows that, considered as a bald proposition, the unheated house is not a very favourable environment. Yet I have seen some very fine crops raised in these conditions, with the aid of a one foot deep hot-bed.

In each case the general cultural programme is similar to that outlined in Chapters XI and XII, and the roots can be planted at the same time. The difference is that there is a one foot deep hot-bed beneath the border, or where the roots are planted in pots or boxes, these receptacles are surrounded by a six-inch layer of hot-bed material. The latter generates the heat and, as I have indicated, grand crops are raised.

HOW TO MAKE THE HOT-BED

The ideal material for hot-bed making is strawy, urine-stained horse manure containing twenty to thirty per cent of droppings. Shake the material, and after mixing thoroughly the droppings and the straw, turn over the heap. Repeat the turning every three days until the temperature, having reached its maximum, falls to seventy-five degrees Fahr., at which level it will remain steady as long as the plants require heat. For the testing of the temperature a plunging thermometer is the best instrument, but where one is not available a sufficiently reliable guide can be obtained by plunging two or three sticks deeply into the centre of the heap, and testing the temperature by handling. When these sticks can be held without the least discomfort, it can be asumed that the temperature stands at seventy-five degrees or thereabouts. During the time the turnings are in progress the heap should be covered with boards if there is no accommodation beneath an open shed.

An equal part mixture of horse manure and leaves also makes a good hot-bed, and will appeal to many in these days, when manure is so scarce. Before starting to turn the ingredients, mix them thoroughly. Afterwards compost them as advised for manure alone.

VEGETABLE SEEDLINGS

Though the vegetable seedlings mentioned in Chapter XIII cannot be sown quite as early in the unheated house, all can be sown the first week in March, or on a later date where, as pointed out in the chapter concerned, this is appropriate. The vigour of seedlings raised in these conditions is unquestionable, and it is surprising how quickly they develop when put out into the open ground. They catch up to those that have had the benefit of artificial heat.

The greatest obstacle is damping off, which takes its chance of attacking when the seedlings are temporarily embarrassed by unpropitious outdoor conditions. That trouble, however, passes by the crops of those who have learned the advantage of using Cheshunt Compound as a preventive. Do, therefore, be specially faithful to this previously described treatment when raising vegetable seedlings without heat.

MISCELLANEOUS CROPS

In Chapter X, I deal with a variety of miscellaneous crops. These can all be raised in the unheated house by methods like those advised in that chapter. In every instance remember that the environment is different and seek, by carefully studied ventilation and cautious watering, to make the absence of artificial heat no disadvantage.

Chapter XVI

THE HEATED FRAME

AS this book is intended to cover faithfully all forms of under-glass culture, I must not omit the heated frame, that is, the frame which is heated by electricity or gas, or through which there runs a system of hot water pipes. Actually, a structure of this kind is a heated glasshouse in miniature, hence I need not deal again with the crops that can be grown in it, the times of sowing, and their general management. For that information I ask my readers to look up the section dealing with crops in the heated glasshouse. As the structure itself is slightly different, I must offer a few observations on ventilating and kindred matters.

VENTILATION

Ventilation in a heated frame is just as essential as in a heated greenhouse, but the volume of heated air is much smaller, and the crops are nearer to the glass. If anything like the same amount of air were given, the thermometer would fall very rapidly, creating one of those violent temperature fluctuations which adversely affect the health of all living things, plants in particular.

The smallness of the volume of air also brings with it the peril of rapid overheating when the sun shines brightly on the glass. More than a little care must be taken, therefore, in the handling of this rather delicate situation. One's own judgment soon gets the right angle. One learns to give less air, but to be ready to give it when the temperature is rising rapidly by sun heat. Wood tilts should be made to lift the lights on the leeward side, thus making sure that cold winds never blow directly on to the plants.

WATERING

The gardener cannot enter a heated frame. He must do all the work from the outside, and the only way in which this can be done is to lift the lights. Obviously caution must be used in doing this. It would be asking for trouble, for instance, to lift the lights and allow an inrush of outside air on a frosty, foggy, or very cold day. Happily during such conditions it is seldom necessary to lift the lights at all, as the crops themselves are in a state of more or less suspended animation in sympathy with outside conditions.

At the same time, even during difficult spells there are intervals when the air clears or warms up. Choose these for watering and other essential attentions. In milder, more summery seasons there are periods which are more genial than the rest. It is helpful to the plants if their requirements can be met at such times. We make a great mistake if we imagine that tropical and temperate or cold conditions can be exchanged at will. The water used for watering must be heated to the temperature of the frame. Where it is practicable, fix a tank in some part of the structure, and always after every watering fill up the tank, so that when next water is required it will be at the right temperature.

Where for any reason a tank cannot be arranged, keep in the frame sufficient pails filled with water or, alternatively, carry to the frame slightly aired water. I have seen so many tragedies resulting from the use of cold water than I do not hesitate to stress this aspect of the management.

ATMOSPHERIC HUMIDITY

The limited atmosphere in a frame is conducive to the rapid drying of the atmosphere in Spring, Summer, and part of Autumn. Unless the condition is corrected by overhead spraying with clear water night and morning, and the use of evaporizing troughs, the air will become so parched that no small part of the management will be that of chasing thrips and red spider and other pests that flourish in the absence of humidity.

The evaporizing trough, by the way, is a trough which fits on to the flow pipe. There should be one every ten feet, and the troughs in the seasons mentioned must be regularly filled with water, the evaporation of which will help atmospheric humidity. During Winter the troughs should not be filled, for in that season sufficient atmospheric humidity is created by the plants themselves through transpiration, or the discharge of watery vapour from the leaves.

PESTS

For some reason that is difficult to explain, certain pests are very troublesome in a heated frame. Amongst these are slugs, which can do a power of damage in a short time. A sharp look out should be kept for them, and when it is found that they are active, make a search, and a good many will be caught red-handed under pots and boxes. A liberal sprinkling of soot, and the setting of Meta fuel and bone meal traps, will quickly clear up those that have eluded the eye of the seeker.

Crickets, cockroaches and wood-lice also flourish about the pipe track. There is less encouragement for them if this part of the structure is not regarded as a dumping ground for dead leaves and other litter. Clean pipe tracks are most hygienic. It does not always follow that when they are maintained these enemies are excluded. Happily they can be exterminated by using the powders that are sold at most garden shops for dealing with wood-lice, cockroaches and crickets.

HOW TO ARRANGE THE FRAME

I know from experience that it is a mistake to have a fixed stage in a heated frame. I inherited such a frame on one occasion, and could not make use of it until I had converted it into a portable stage. In one part of the season, for instance, the frame might be filled with lettuce, a dwarf-growing crop that should be as near the light as possible consistent with the leaves clearing the glass. In another part of the season the frame might be full of French beans, tall-growing plants that would have no chance at all on a stage that gave happy conditions to lettuce.

Thus, when the stage is portable it can be brought in for the dwarf growers, and when it is desired to grow something tall the stage can be taken out, making room for the plants in the well of the frame. A lattice stage is better than a close board or tile stage. The water drips through to the well quickly, creating pleasant humidity beneath the pots or boxes.

Chapter XVII

THE COLD FRAME

THERE are few gardeners and allotment holders who do not possess a cold frame. I dissent from the oft-repeated statement that this is the poor man's form of under-glass gardening, though I do recognize that many a man who cannot afford a greenhouse can and does afford a cold frame. This structure should, however, be in the equipment of every garden, large and small.

METHOD OF CONSTRUCTION

On this point a great deal might be said, but it would not be wise to lay down hard and fast rules regarding size. I do consider, however, that a light five feet long by three feet wide is about as heavy as any man feels

POTATOES IN COLD FRAME

inclined to lift. There is also the further consideration that accidents will happen, and that if anything untoward occurs to a very large light, the financial loss is heavy.

The slope of the light is a matter of considerable moment. In a sharply sloping frame the temperature rises too quickly for the welfare of the crops. The slope should be gradual, say about thirty degrees, thus securing the maximum practical benefit from the sun's heat, combined with safety. The very flat light traps too little heat, and does not, therefore, make use of the gardener's most valuable ally.

A frame having brick or concrete sides is more durable than one having wood sides, though against this must be arrayed the disadvantage of immobility. A concrete or brick-sided frame is a fixture, whereas a wood frame can be moved at will, and sometimes there is an advantage in movement.

Of the two materials, concrete and brick, the latter is the better, because brick absorbs heat during the day and gives it out at night, whereas concrete is stone cold all the time. Where wood is used, this must be thoroughly seasoned or it will soon decay. At one time red deal was greatly favoured for frame-making, but red cedar is superseding it as being a more durable proposition.

THE TURF FRAME

The frame with turf sides is quite as successful for crop growing as one having brick, concrete or wood sides, and the turves, if bonded like a bricklayer bonds or crosses his bricks, will last many years without admitting so much as the suspicion of a draught. An appropriate back height is thirty inches, an appropriate front height twenty-seven inches. The length and width of the frame will be determined by the dimensions of the lights that are fitted on to it.

THE POSITION OF THE FRAME

Where there is a greenhouse, an excellent position for the frame or frames is on the sunny side of it. The frame gathers some reflected heat, and in that way benefits. As it is customary to move plants out of the greenhouse into the frame, and vice versa, this can be done with the minimum labour, and the minimum risk to the plants, when the two structures are in juxtaposition.

Where there is no greenhouse select a sunny situation, if possible, sheltered from cold winds, which in Winter and Spring are often so penetrating that they materially lower the temperature in the frame.

WATERING AND VENTILATING

Much of what I said regarding watering and ventilating the heated frame applies with equal force here. Of course, it is understood that as there is no artificial heat to dry up the moisture, the volume of water required in all but the warmest weather will be considerably less. But do choose the best times for watering, thus avoiding the unnecessary introduction of a chilling air. And always, from the beginning of October until the end of March, water in a morning, so that the atmosphere has a chance to dry up before night. Adopt precisely similar ventilating principles to those outlined for the heated frame.

WINTER PROTECTION

Plants that are wintered in a cold frame must obviously possess a considerable degree of hardiness, or they would have no hope of survival. At the same time it is not advisable to subject them to the lowest temperatures. Even if they survive these they will not do as well as if some protection is given.

This should take the form of covering the glass on frosty nights with the regulation fibre mats, sacks, coco matting, or some material equal to turning a frost. Spread the mats all over the glass, and if there is a likelihood of wind, lay boards across the frame to prevent the covers from blowing off.

As these covers completely exclude light, they bring the possibility of evil with the good they certainly do. By that I mean that if the covers are left in position after the frost departs, the plants beneath will spindle. Do take them off at the appropriate time, therefore, and open them out somewhere so that they have a chance to dry before they are required again.

WIND DAMAGE

Wind can do a great deal of damage to a cold frame. If, for example, a pane of glass is broken, or in some way the wind gets under the lights, it will lift them like pieces of matchwood, and when at last they find terra-firma their condition can be better imagined than described.

PEAS GROWING IN COLD FRAME.   FOR PLANTING OUT

Avoid the possibility of damage on this scale by fixing catches on each running rail that holds the lights.   These catches are screwed down and turned over the lights when there is risk of wind.   Now that we have considered the general aspect of frame management, we can deal with crops that can be grown or partially grown in a cold frame.   In cases where box cultivation is suggested, use the type of box and the compost advised in Chapter XIII.

PEAS AND BROAD BEANS

Set the broad bean seed three inches apart, the pea seed two inches, and just cover them with compost. Mid-January to mid-February, according to the weather, is a good time for this work. Do not water until the seedlings show, and moderately afterwards. Too much moisture is conducive to sappy growth. The seedlings will be ready for transplanting to the open garden in April, the

AN EARLY BATCH OF BROAD BEANS RAISED IN COLD FRAME, FINISHING OFF OUTDOORS

beans being set out alternately in a double row at six inches apart, the peas in a triple row at three inches apart. Both crops will give specially early yields.

THE CABBAGE FAMILY

Brussels sprouts, cabbages and cauliflowers intended for mid-June planting will be in fine condition for the purpose if sown in boxes in the cold frame in mid-March. When the seedlings are big enough to handle, transplant them at two inches apart into other boxes, selecting the sturdiest seedlings, and hardening off well before the final planting.

ONIONS

Onions sown in the cold frame after the New Year starts seldom make big enough plants by the time they must be set out in the garden to justify the labour involved, but splendid results are obtained when the seed is sown in September. Keep the boxes well up to the light during Winter, transplant the seedlings at two inches apart into other boxes in February, and they will be ready to go out by the end of April. Choose varieties that are not likely to run to seed quickly, such as Autumn Queen and Ebenezer.

CELERY, CELERIAC AND LEEKS

If these crops are sown in boxes in early March, and the seedlings pricked out into other boxes at two inches apart when they are big enough to handle, they will be ready for the open garden by the end of June, an appropriate time for setting out a second batch. It is advisable, before sowing celery and celeriac, to steep the seed overnight in water, to expedite germination.

SUMMER CAULIFLOWERS

Some of the finest Summer cauliflowers are grown with the protecting aid of the cold frame. The method is to sow the seed out of doors in late August in half an inch deep drills spaced six inches apart, transplanting the seedlings into boxes at three inches apart when they are big enough to handle. During Winter give as much light as the season allows, and if there is the slightest sign of White Rust on the leaves, dispose of this disease by dusting with flowers of sulphur. The plants are ready for their permanent positions in early April. The variety May Queen is perfect for this sowing.

WINTER PARSLEY

Fresh parsley may be had throughout Winter by broad-casting thinly in early July seed of the variety Myatt's Garnishing, just covering it by light raking. When the plants have formed three or four leaves, set them out at six inches apart in boxes, and every three weeks, or as near thereto as moisture is required, water with lime water (one ounce in two gallons of water). There is nothing like lime for helping Winter parsley to crop well.

CAULIFLOWERS WINTERED IN COLD FRAME. READY FOR PLANTING OUT

WINTER LETTUCE

By Winter lettuce is not necessarily meant lettuce that matures during official Winter. Only in very favourable seasons does this happen, but splendid heads of the variety May Queen will be ready for cutting in April if seed is sown out of doors the third week in August in half an inch deep drills spaced four inches apart. Set out the seedlings at eight inches apart in boxes when they are in their fourth normal leaf. Give all the light possible, ventilate as generously as the season allows, dust with derris powder if there are signs of green-fly, and with flowers of sulphur or green sulphur powder if the purplish-white blotches indicative of Mildew develop.

TOMATOES

Tomatoes are a profitable crop in the cold frame in Summer. They should not, however, be planted until the third week in May, for they suffer in the low temperatures from which we are not certain to escape until that season. Happily the frame has then been cleared of crops that are to be planted out, and the tomatoes make a useful succession.

Varieties such as Kondine Red and Sunrise do specially well. They can be planted in continuous borders at the bottom of the frame, similar to those advised for greenhouse tomatoes. One matter is very important, namely, that of making the frame accessible at all times. There must be no difficulty in pushing the lights up or down as required. To this end it is advisable to screw holdfasts into the runners at a foot apart from the top to the bottom of the frame, thread wires through them, and tie the tomatoes to the wires. There is then no impediment to the free movement of the lights. In other respects the treatment is quite orthodox for tomatoes as described earlier in this book.

VEGETABLE MARROWS, GOURDS, SQUASHES

In Chapter VI, I described the cultivation of these crops, which are equally suitable for cultivation in the cold frame. They can be sown in mid-May and, like tomatoes, provide a profitable way of using the frame in Summer. Set two seeds at four inches apart and half an inch deep near the centre of twelve inch wide, nine inch high mounds of compost, one mound to the light. Later reduce the seedlings to one per mound. On the formation of the sixth leaf remove the growing points of the plants, to encourage side shoots. Take out the growing points of the fruit-bearing side shoots two leaves beyond the fruit, those of the non-bearing side shoots just above the seventh leaf. In this way the plants which, of course, adopt a trailing habit, are kept within reasonable bounds. Remove the lights when more room is required, and allow the growth to overflow. In other respects the cultural attentions are similar to those advised for these crops in the green-house, and similar varieties may be grown.

CARROTS IN COLD FRAME

CUCUMBERS AND MELONS

The chances with cucumbers and melons in the cold frame are not quite so certain as are those with marrows, gourds and squashes, because they are tenderer. Never-theless, if seed is sown as advised for these three crops, but in early June, the results will be very encouraging in a good season. Remove the growing points of both the cucumbers and the melons as advised for vegetable marrows, but do not take off the lights. The plants must be covered all the time. The cucumber Conqueror and the melon Munro's Little Heath are ideal for frame culture.

MISCELLANEOUS CROPS

Early yields of the following crops can be obtained in the cold frame : carrot, Early Horn ; turnip, White Model ; spinach, Victoria ; beet, Crimson Globe ; lettuce, Tom Thumb ; radish, French Breakfast ; and salad onion, Spring Bunching. In late February spread at the bottom of the frame a three inch layer of rubble for drainage, covering this with a five inch layer of good, sifted garden soil. Place the lights on for a fortnight, to give the soil a chance to warm up and dry out a little.

Then in half an inch deep drills at six inches apart sow all but the radishes and onions, which should be broadcasted on the surface, and raked in. Now close the lights until the seedlings appear, after which ventilation should be given as the weather allows. Thin all the crops sufficiently to allow room for proper development, water carefully, and there will be splendid returns.

Chapter XVIII

CLOCHE GARDENING

THERE has been a great increase in cloche gardening in recent years. To give an example, there are now more than twenty thousand members of the Cloche Guild, and the membership roll is increasing daily. It is most essential, therefore, that cloche gardening should be dealt with in this book.

First of all it might be advisable to define cloches. I think the Americans have hit on a very happy description. They call them miniature greenhouses, and this, in fact, is what cloches are. They are sheets of glass held in position by a skilfully devised system of wires. There are many patterns, each specially adapted for certain types of culture.

FROST WILL NOT HARM THESE CLOCHED STRAWBERRY FLOWERS

CLOCHE TYPES

First there are the Tent types—small, medium and long. Each is composed of two sheets of glass, the diameter being eleven to fifteen inches, the height from the soil to the ridge seven to nine inches. In view of the comparatively limited head room, these cloches are admirably adapted for the cultivation of dwarf crops such as lettuce, radishes, shorthorn carrots, and so on, though they can be used to give protection to taller crops for a time. Later, taller cloches can be put over these crops, or if the weather is suitable they can be exposed completely.

Secondly there are the Barn types, which give more head room, varying from twelve to nineteen inches, according to the type. Beneath these cloches many crops, such as early dwarf peas, Dwarf Fan broad beans, early potatoes, turnips, beet, asparagus, strawberries, raspberries (the canes being trained horizontally) can be brought to maturity very much earlier than would be the case if they were grown without protection.

Such crops as outdoor tomatoes, vegetable marrows, ridge cucumbers, melons, sweet corn, egg plants, and many others can be sown early under Barn cloches, and protected during critical weather. Not only are they ready for use earlier, but the yield and quality are much superior to those of purely outdoor produce.

Finally there is the Tomato T cloche, with twenty-two inches of head room, a roof glass sheet measuring twenty-four inches by nine inches, and side sheets measuring twenty-four inches long. This comparatively new cloche gives unrivalled facilities for making an outstanding success of tomatoes.

ERECTING AND HANDLING CLOCHES

The makers of cloches give full instructions regarding assembly. This is such a simple matter that he who runs may read. A few minutes' practice is sufficient to qualify anyone as an assembler, and it will be found that the assembled cloche is so rigid that it can be moved anywhere without the least risk of glass breakage.

Of course, it is not in the interests of good garden working to be carrying cloches all round the place frequently. Far better so to arrange the scheme that when the cloches have fulfilled their function over one crop they can be transferred to a near-by site for another.

If they must be moved a considerable distance, a hand barrow arranged on the stretcher principle is a good and successful method of transport.

PREPARATION OF THE SOIL

Owing to the rapidity with which crops mature under cloches, it is possible to get three or four crops a year. Clearly if this excellent result is to be achieved, the ground must be dressed generously with manure or compost at least once a year. One two-gallon pailful of either should be incorporated with each square yard. Where neither manure nor compost is available, a one pound per square yard dressing of peat, supplemented by a two ounce per square yard helping of a balanced artificial fertilizer (both to be raked in) may be used as a substitute. Further, there are proprietary organic manure substitutes, and if these are used in accordance with the maker's instructions, they will give a good account of themselves. Cloche crops, like all other crops, benefit by feeding during the growing season.

WARMING THE SOIL

Even in the coldest weather the atmospheric temperature under cloches is considerably higher than it is out of doors. In fact, it can safely be said that these covers will resist twelve degrees of frost. Atmospheric temperature does not, however, constitute all in the way of an environment that a plant requires. The soil temperature must bear the right relationship to that of the atmosphere, and this can only be if the cloches are placed in position some time before the crop is sown or planted. The actual period varies according to the season and, to some extent, the crop.

In Winter cover for three weeks, in Spring for a fortnight, at other periods a week. In addition to warming up the soil, pre-covering does at certain times allow the soil to get rid of superfluous water, thus enabling it to be worked into a kindly condition. In dry periods the ground should be well watered before it is covered.

ARRANGING THE CLOCHES

I do not propose to make a hard and fast line with regard to this matter, as I realize that in spite of the advantages of proximity in the cloched areas, there are some gardeners who will wish to move their covers about freely. There are, however, one or two points that call for attention, because they are of universal application.

As cloches are traps to catch sunbeams, it follows that they should be placed in a light position where there are sunbeams to trap. Experience and experiment suggest that when the cloches run east and west, they get greater benefit from the light and warmth than they do in any other situation. In most gardens it is possible to give this aspect without in any way interfering with the cropping arrangement.

Before the cloches are put down, the ground should be made reasonably firm and thoroughly level. Only in such conditions can the base of the cloches be made to fit flush with the soil. They must do this, or the draughts that enter will, to a large extent, neutralize the effect of the sunbeams that are trapped.

CLOCHES ARE CONTINUOUS

With the exception that when a single cloche is closed at both ends and made into a miniature seed-bed, cloches are continuous, by which I mean that one fits to the end of the other, making an unbroken row of the desired length. See to it that this row is unbroken by making the cloches fit end to end, unless some air is required, when they can be opened out. Where two rows of cloches are run side by side (and this is a space and labour-saving device), allow four to six inches between each two rows, and use that valuable protected strip for the cultivation of early radishes and lettuce.

Where two or more blocks of two rows are run side by side, leave a two feet wide path between each two blocks, to allow for the necessary cultural attentions. It will be realized that when a row of cloches has been put down, complete top and side cover has been given, except at the ends, which are still open. If these are left open in any but warm weather, the row of cloches will act like a tunnel. Cold air will sweep in at one end and out at the other, with unfortunate consequences to the crops underneath.

For this reason at all times when complete protection is desirable, fix a glass sheet at each end of each row, thus excluding the cold draughts. Prevent these glass sheets from chattering in the wind, and possibly getting broken, by pushing in a substantial stake near each sheet of glass. Press it well up to exclude air, and tie the top of the stake to the nearest cloche ring. This entirely prevents movement.

VENTILATING

Cloches are provided with an ingenious self-ventilating arrangement which in cold weather renders any attention on the part of the gardener unnecessary. As Spring advances, however, and the days become warmer, more air is required. The extent to which this should be given is largely a matter on which the individual should consult his own judgment. No wise person will attempt to give unalterable rules on ventilation, but this can be said as a general guide. When more air is required, open each two cloches one, two, three, four, inches, or even more or, alternatively, take out every third, fourth or fifth cloche. When ventilating commences, it will be essential to replace or close up the cloches at night, but later in the season they may be, and often are, left open as a preliminary to taking them off altogether.

The Tomato T cloches are provided with a special ventilating arrangement. By means of a twisted and graduated wire, it is possible progressively to open one of the side glasses, or to remove this side glass altogether.

SHOWING HOW TO WATER CLOCHE CROPS

WATERING AND FEEDING

Considerable misapprehension exists regarding the amount of water needed by crops under cloches. Indeed, some people imagine that there is so much labour of this kind that they hesitate to become users of these excellent covers. May I give the right perspective ? Water is the first need of all plant life, and there are times when crops under cloches must have it. But generally they need only be watered when crops growing out of doors must be watered also.

The arrangements for the transmission of water in soil are such that equilibrium is set up. Thus, if the soil outside cloches is moister than that beneath them, these forces will get to work and equalize the position. When watering is necessary, take out a four inch wide, four inch deep channel alongside each row of cloches, pour the

CLOCHES STACKED WHEN NOT IN USE

water into that and allow it to make its own way underneath. On no account should the cloches be lifted off unless, of course, the weather is warm enough to allow for this to be done without a damaging inrush of cold air.

When the time for feeding comes, let the food reach the crops in the same way. If liquids are used, pour them into the channel, if artificials, spread them in the channel and pour water on to them.

SHADING

There are periods when very hot, bright sun embarrasses crops under cloches. Newly transplanted subjects and small seedlings sometimes feel it, while cucumbers and melons in the normal course of cultivation require slight shade. This can be given very quickly and effectively by spraying the glass with lime-wash through a syringe or rosed watering can. The lime-wash must, of course, be passed through a hair sieve or a bit of fine muslin to take out the grit.

STORING CLOCHES

Though cloches can profitably be used all the year round, the occasion may arise when it is desired to lay them aside for a short period. Don't dis-assemble them, but tuck them one inside the other, and arrange the nest of cloches on firm boards or a bit of old sacking, to prevent weeds from growing amongst them and fouling the glass. Take care not to arrange them near a wall or fence, otherwise cats or dogs might use them as a jumping board and break the glass.

Chapter XIX

CROPS UNDER CLOCHES

POD-BEARING CROPS

BROAD BEANS. Sow in mid-January in the South, the end of January in the Midlands, and early February in the North, using tall cloches. Make the drills three inches deep and nine inches wide. In the drill sow two rows of seed alternately at nine inches apart, with a few extra seeds at the end of the row to provide plants for gap-filling. The cloches should be removed when more head room is required, and the tops of the plants taken out when five clusters of bloom have shown on each. For this sowing Johnson's Wonderful is an excellent variety. The crop should be ready for gathering from the middle to the end of May.

PEAS UNDER CLOCHES

The same variety may also be sown in mid-February and March, while in early April a good Windsor sort such as Harlington Green may be put in. These later sowings, after they are uncloched, may be attacked by Black-fly. If they are, destroy the pest by dusting with derris powder.

PEAS. January and February are good pea-sowing months, mid-January for the South, the end of the month in the Midlands, and early February in the North. A second sowing may be made in the South in mid-February, and at the end of the month in both the Midlands and the North. For these sowings choose a quick-maturing sort such as the eighteen inch tall Kelvedon Wonder.

In March another sowing may be made in all districts, this time selecting a variety like the two and a half feet tall Giant Stride. In April and May sow maincrop varieties, like the five feet tall Alderman, one sowing each month. In June follow up with Kelvedon Wonder again for September and October picking. In early October in the Midlands and North, and in early November in the South, sow a hardy sort like Meteor (one foot) for gathering the following May. The January and February sowings are ready in June, after which there is a steady succession of peas from later cloche sowings and those sown in the open garden.

The Autumn, January and February batches will finish under the cloches, but the others will need to be uncovered when they nearly touch the glass. Sow all batches of peas in eight inch wide drills two inches deep in heavy soil, and three inches in light. Set the seed three inches apart. As mice sometimes burrow under the cloches, it is advisable to keep an eye on the situation, and set traps if the need arises. Use barn cloches for peas.

DWARF BEANS. These include both haricots and the dwarf French type, the pods of which are used fresh. Make several sowings of the French type under barn cloches, as these afford this tender crop full protection for the maximum period right through if necessary. Make the first sowing in the South in mid-March, the end of the month in the Midlands, and early April in the North. The crop will be ready for pulling in June and early July, according to the sowing time. After the end of March sow fortnightly in all parts of the country until the end of May, after which French beans may safely be sown out of doors.

Mid-April is a suitable time to sow haricots in all districts, and in view of the fact that ripe seed is the aim, it is helpful to leave the crop under cover all the time. When sowing both French and haricot beans, take out a two inch deep, six inch wide drill, and set one row of seed down the centre at nine inches apart. A few extra seeds at the end of the drill will provide plants for filling up vacant places.

DWARF FRENCH BEANS UNDER CLOCHES

Both these crops are great moisture lovers and should, therefore, be copiously watered in dry weather. If Autumn is unpropitious, cover the late outdoor-sown batches, and the crop will mature perfectly. When the pods of haricots turn brown, the crop is ready for harvesting. At that stage pull up the plants, lay them

EARLY HEALTHY RUNNER BEANS.   RAISED UNDER CLOCHES

139

down under the cloches, and in about a week the seed will be as perfectly ripe as haricots can be, and will constitute a splendid food reserve for the Winter. An excellent variety of dwarf French bean is The Prince, of haricot Brown Dutch.

RUNNER BEANS. A much-treasured crop, but owing to its tropical origin very chancy out of doors. It is, however, a conspicuous success if sown under tall cloches early in April in the South, mid-April in the Midlands, and the end of the month in the North. The crop is ready for gathering in July, and continues until frosts come. Of course, the cloches must be taken off and the plants staked when more growing space is required. Set the beans in a double row down the centre of the cloches at two inches deep and nine inches apart. If the seeds are set opposite each other, staking will be much easier. It is necessary to watch for Black-fly, which on leaving broad beans often attacks this crop in force. An application of derris powder will destroy it. Any difficulty about the setting of the early flowers will be overcome by spraying the plants daily when they are in bloom.

THE CABBAGE FAMILY

BRUSSELS SPROUTS. Two batches of this crop are grown in most gardens. Both can be raised under tent or small cloches, the first at the end of January in the South, mid-February in the Midlands, and the end of that month in the North. The seedlings from this batch will be ready for their final quarters from early to mid-May, according to the season and district.

Sow one month later in all districts for moving to the final quarters one month later than the periods given above. It is desirable to make a specially fine seed bed for small seeds such as this. The drills should be half an inch deep and three inches apart. If the seeds are spaced half an inch apart (and this is a good way) they can go straight to the final quarters. It will not be necessary to set them out in nursery beds. If they are sown thickly they must be transplanted into nursery beds at four inches apart, and cloche cover will be necessary if this is done before the third week in April. As an early Brussels sprout I have every confidence in The Wroxton, while as a late there is nothing better than Cambridge No. 5.

CABBAGES. It is customary to grow three batches of cabbages—early Summer, late Summer and Spring. All can be assisted by cloches. I will treat the batches separately, to avoid confusion. For the early Summer batch Primo is unexcelled. Sow it in late January in the South, mid-February in the Midlands, and the end of the month in the North.

For the late Summer batch sow in mid-March in all districts, choosing a variety like Winningstadt. The procedure in both cases is similar to that advocated for Brussels sprouts. Two batches of Spring cabbages should be sown, one at the end of July, the other in mid-August. Harbinger is appropriate for the first sowing, Offenham for the second. Sow both in the open in half an inch deep drills at six inches apart. After transferring the plants to the final quarters in October, cover them with cloches, and they will be rendered immune from the vicissitudes of wintry weather. This is particularly valuable in the North, where the crop often suffers so much. It is possible, owing to the protection, to cut beautiful cabbages in March and April, whereas in the open, if the plants survive, nothing will be ready for fully six weeks after the dates given.

CAULIFLOWERS. These are difficult to grow, but the use of cloches overcomes many of the difficulties. The first batch, for planting out in April, can be sown in the North in early September, in the Midlands the middle of the month, and in the South at the end. If possible mix some riddled old potting soil with the seed-bed, to give the seedlings a real good chance. Space the seed singly an inch apart in half an inch deep drills set four inches apart. The seedlings will not require moving until they go to their permanent quarters. During Winter keep the glass clean, stir the soil occasionally, and in very severe weather throw sacks or matting over the cloches.

In the middle of January in the South, at the end of the month in the Midlands, and in early February in the North, sow another batch under similar conditions for following the September-sown batch. The latter will be ready for cutting in June, the batch with which I am dealing in July, and another batch, to be sown in March, will mature in August. For the first two sowings the variety Early Erfurt is splendid, as is Snowball for January and February, and Majestic for March.

Specially early cauliflowers may be had from the September-sown lot by allowing them to mature under barn cloches. The ground should, as I have indicated in a previous chapter, be covered a fortnight before planting.

SALAD CROPS

LETTUCE. This health-giving salad is specially successful under cloches, the type known as the low barn being the best, though the tent type can be used with good effect, too. For cutting in October sow the variety May Queen or May King in half an inch deep drills spaced eight inches apart, to which distance the seedlings must later be thinned. Do not, however, hurry with the thinning. Allow the plants to stand as long as they will without congestion before reducing their numbers.

During Winter keep the soil well stirred, and dust with derris powder if there are any signs of green-fly. With no more attention than this, magnificent heads will be ready for cutting at the period mentioned. Alternatively, the seed may be sown under low tent cloches, or in a separate cloche seed-bed such as I described in Chapter XVIII, and be transplanted at eight inches apart under barn cloches in January or February, according to the weather.

LETTUCE THAT MAKES THE MOUTH WATER

Sow again in mid-January in the South, early February in the Midlands, and mid-February in the North, for cutting in May. All the Year Round is a reliable variety for this sowing. Another sowing, this time of All the Year Round or Wonderful, may be made in March and April, for succession cuttings. The plants from the two last-named sowings may require watering, as frequently very dry weather overtakes them.

In the North sow in the open ground at the end of July, in the Midlands the first week in August, in the South the second week in August, for cutting in November.

The variety All the Year Round is the one to sow at this period. In early October cover the plants with cloches, and they will be ready for cutting in November. Lettuce can be associated with other crops under cloches, but I propose to deal with them separately.

THE LADY WITH THE LETTUCE

144

RADISHES. In the South and the mild areas in other parts of the country, radishes may be sown every ten days from early September until mid-April, and they will provide an unbroken succession of this popular salad from early October until June, after which the year's supply can be made up from outdoor sowings. The variety Sparkler is an appropriate choice. Radishes can be grown under any type of cloches. There is room for one row under the small tent. Under the larger types space the rows four inches apart, sowing the seed thinly in half an inch deep drills. Guard against over-crowding, as this is fatal with the radish crop. If the seedlings are singled to two inches apart, every plant will make a good root.

ENDIVE. Very high quality produce is secured under cloches, and this is often difficult out of doors. Make the first sowing of a moss curled variety in the open about the middle of June for cutting in October. Make the drills three-quarters of an inch deep and nine inches apart, thinning to this distance as the need becomes evident. Sow a similar variety a month later for cutting in November, and in August sow a Batavian type in drills one foot apart, thinning to the same distance. All the batches must be covered the third or last week in September, and each batch should be blanched when the plants are about eight inches tall. The leaves may be tied up as endive outdoors is tied up, but the latest tests show that blanching is better, and that there is not the least damping, when the cloches are whitewashed. It should be stated that endive is a great moisture-loving plant, and that when dry weather occurs in the early stages, copious supplies of water should be given.

SALAD ONIONS. The salad onions White Lisbon and Spring Bunching give particularly succulent " white tails " under cloches. Three batches should be sown, the first in August in the Midlands and South, and in

July in the North, for pulling in February and March; the second in mid-February in all districts for gathering in May and June; the third in March for gathering in July and August. For this crop the soil should be firm and fine, and the seed should be broadcasted fairly thickly and raked in. After sowing, sprinkle a little lime on the surface, and if weeds appear before or with the seedlings remove them, as broad-leaved weeds quickly overwhelm narrow-leaved onions. Cover the batches sown in July and August in early October. It is advisable to give these a few weeks in the open though, of course, the other sowings must be made under cloches, and the crops are never uncovered.

The pickling onion The Pearl is included here, as it is difficult to find a better classification for it. Sow in all districts in mid-March, and uncloche the crop in late May. Follow the method advised for salad onions. When the bulbs show signs of ripening, pull them up, lay them on the soil, re-cover with cloches, and in a few days the little bulbs will be thoroughly ripe. Large tent and low barn cloches are suitable for salad and pickling onions.

CUCUMBERS. Long Green and Bedfordshire Prize are two outstanding ridge cucumbers for cloche culture. The Short Prickly Gherkin also does well. All are happy under the low barn type. The seed may be sown in mid-April in the South, at the end of the month in the Midlands, and in early May in the North. With the seed-bed mix a good quantity of leaf mould or peat, and fix up a seed-bed cloche as advised in Chapter XVIII.

Set the seed half an inch deep and two inches apart, pressing it in edgeways with the finger-tips, thus ensuring the development of a perfect seedling. On the formation of the second or third normal leaf, transfer the plants to stations set three feet apart, and previously prepared on the following lines. At each station take out a hole big enough to hold a pailful of manure or compost well pressed down, and a six-inch layer of good soil, the latter not to rise above soil level. This is important, as the space must not be taken up by mounds.

A BRACE OF CUCUMBERS UNDER CLOCHES

On the formation of the fifth leaf, take out the growing point of each plant to induce side shoots, after which no stopping will be necessary. The appetite of cucumbers for water is well known, and I stress the need for faithful attention in this matter. Water copiously in dry weather. Unless the plants make specially vigorous growth, barn cloches will provide enough room for them, and with ventilation on the lines advised in Chapter XVIII will

HEALTHY BEET BENEATH CLOCHES

contribute to a great crop. It will, however, be necessary to shade, as cucumber leaves " scald " when the sun shines directly on to them through clear glass.

An alternative method of culture is to set out greenhouse-raised plants under the cloches in early May. Being more advanced than cloche-raised seedlings, they yield cucumbers sooner, but that is the only advantage they possess. As there are often many salad days in late Spring and early Summer, the gain is one that might appeal.

BEET. In the variety Crimson Globe there is a first-class beet for salad purposes. It can be sown in the South at the end of February, in mid-March in the Midlands, and at the end of the month in the North. In all districts sow a second batch three weeks later for succession. The large tent cloche is eminently suitable for one row, while the low barn type takes three rows at eight inches apart. Uncloche the second batch when the leaves get near the glass. The first batch will be ready in June.

The so-called seed of beet is in reality a type of fruit called a capsule. It contains from three to five seeds. For this reason anything like thick sowing constitutes a great waste, and, in addition, there is the risk of over-crowding the seedlings. Cover these matters by sowing two seeds (or more properly capsules) at four inches apart in one inch deep drills, afterwards thinning to one seedling per station. On the formation of the second or third normal leaf, give a one ounce per yard run dressing of agricultural salt, which ministers to a fundamental need and greatly improves the results.

ROOT CROPS

SHORTHORN CARROTS. The shorthorn carrots Early Horn and Early Nantes, sown in mid-January in the South, the end of the month in the Midlands, and early February in the North, will yield splendid roots for gathering in May and June. Repeat sowings may be made in the Midlands and South in August for pulling in Autumn. The large tent type of cloche answers well, for it will accommodate two rows at six inches apart. The barn type holds four rows at five inches apart and, of course, allows a little more top space. To ensure an even and fairly thin distribution of seed, mix with the latter an equal quantity of dry sand. Make the drills half an inch deep. The seedlings will not require thinning unless there is clear evidence of overcrowding.

MAINCROP CARROTS. The maincrop carrot James's Intermediate can be lifted full-size in June and July if sown in all districts in mid-February in drills

CARROTS COMING FORWARD UNDER CLOCHES

standing nine inches apart. The seedlings should be thinned to six inches, and the cloches, if they are not required for any other purpose, might well remain over the crop all the time, as they are a wonderful safeguard against Carrot Fly attack. Incidentally, maincrop carrots raised in this way possess a juiciness and flavour that must be tested to be believed.

If maincrop carrots are sown in early August and cloched (with ventilation) all the time, they will yield a splendid crop for lifting in November or December. This is an excellent crop to succeed early peas or broad beans.

ONIONS. Cloches open the way to success with this very much treasured crop. It is recognized, for instance, that transplanted seedlings make specially fine bulbs. They can, from end of January sowings in the Midlands and South, and early February sowings in the North, be raised for moving to their permanent quarters at the appointed season, and fine sturdy plants they will be. The varieties Ailsa Craig and Premier are all that could be desired.

Make the drills half an inch deep and five inches apart, sowing very thinly. It is even worth while to space the seed an inch apart, to ensure seedlings of the best possible calibre. Varieties such as Bedfordshire Champion and James's Keeping may be sown in mid-February in all districts in the positions in which they are to mature. Make the drills ten inches apart, and later thin the seedlings to six inches. Take off the cloches at the end of April or early May, according to the weather. Bring them into use again for ripening the bulbs after they are lifted. Spread them in a single row under the cloches until nobody can doubt that they are thoroughly ripe. In recent years many outdoor-ripened onions have gone bad in store. There is no record of a cloche-ripened stock having done this.

In August sow in half an inch deep drills at a foot apart, in fairly rich, firm soil, a proven Autumn onion such as Autumn Queen. In October cover the rows with barn cloches, and keep these over the plants until the following April, when they should be transplanted at nine inches apart, or thinned to a similar distance and uncloched. Anyone who tries that method with Autumn onions will agree that no other programme can equal it.

CELERIAC. This is the turnip-rooted celery, a crop with which many people would like to excel. To do this sow under large tent cloches at the end of February in the South, early March in the Midlands, and the end of March in the North in a well prepared seed-bed beneath a barn cloche. Broadcast the seed very thinly, and sprinkle on top of it a quarter of an inch layer of finely sifted soil. If the seedlings are too thick, thin them, so that all have room for development, transplanting the thinnings under other cloches. The seedlings will be ready for their final move from the middle to the end of May, according to the weather. If they are planted in rich soil at one foot apart, fed generously with weak liquid manure and are relieved of their side shoots, they will make roots of maximum size.

POTATOES. New potatoes in May are a prospect that pleases. This prospect will be translated into reality if sprouted tubers of the variety May Queen are planted in mid-February in the South, the end of the month in the Midlands, and early March in the North. Reduce the sprouts to two per tuber, and plant the tubers a foot apart in four-inch deep drills lined with leaf mould or peat. Vhen growth is seven or eight inches tall, earth up the stems with four inches of fine soil. Tall barn cloches are the best for this crop, but the crop can be started under large tents, these being replaced by barns later.

TURNIPS. Low barn cloches can be used to advantage for early turnip growing. Sow the variety Early White

TOMATOES PLANTED UNDER CLOCHES, AND STILL PARTIALLY PROTECTED
BY THEM

Milan in the South in early March, in the Midlands at the middle of the month, and in the North at the end. The roots will be ready for pulling in May and June. For succession sow a batch in all districts three weeks later. Make the drills one inch deep and eight inches apart, afterwards thinning the seedlings to this distance.

In early September again sow White Milan for pulling young in November, and in early September also cover the Winter variety Manchester Market sown a month earlier. Vinter turnips grown under cloches are very succulent, and are not liable to heart rot.

MISCELLANEOUS CROPS

TOMATOES. In any but a favourable season purely outdoor tomatoes are an uncertain crop. A spell of cold, wet weather may ruin the prospects. That is why tomato growing under cloches, which gives such heavy yields in all types of season, is becoming so popular. The procedure is as follows. Sow at the end of March in the South, early April in the Midlands, mid-April in the North, selecting a good variety such as Harbinger or Pride of the Garden. Prepare the seed-bed carefully, making the soil fine, and sow the seed one and a half inches apart and three-quarters of an inch deep under a large barn cloche.

When the seedlings are big enough to handle, transplant them under similar cloches at three inches apart, or alternatively and preferably, set them separately in small cardboard pots, arranging these in little trenches. The pot method involves less risk of root disturbance at the final planting time. Set out the plants at eighteen inches apart in six-inch deep, nine-inch wide trenches from the middle to the end of May, having previously manured the trenches generously. Allow each plant to carry one basal side shoot, training this at an angle of forty-five degrees. That side shoot will carry one or two trusses of fruit, the main stem three or four, in accordance with the vigour of the plant.

Liberal watering and feeding are necessary, and the plants must be securely staked and tied, and also have every side shoot save the retained one removed. Now two methods may be followed. Those who have the tall T type of cloche can keep the plants under all the time and, of course, this means more fruit, for the conditions are protected. Ample facilities exist for ventilating this type of cloche.

Alternatively, where large barns are employed, the cloches may be taken off when more head room is needed, and given open air treatment for a few weeks. In early September take out the stakes, lay the plants on peat or straw, and re-cover them with the cloches, under which the fruit will ripen perfectly.

Another way with the barn cloches is to train the plants on horizontally placed strings or wires, and ventilate them by opening out the cloches as required. This is a good method, especially for those who, owing to geographical limitations, hesitate to give full exposure, even for a short period.

SWEET CORN. Sweet corn is rapidly becoming a popular crop in Great Britain. Being on the tender side, outdoor sowings cannot be made very early. If seedlings are raised in the greenhouse and planted out, they do not always get away well, for sweet corn is averse to transplanting. For these reasons cloches present a unique opportunity. There are two sections, early and late. If both are sown, there will be a succession from July until October. The John Innes Hybrid is a good early sort, Golden Bantam a reliable late.

Sow both sections early in April in the South, mid-April in the Midlands, the last week in the North. Set the seed three inches apart and an inch deep, one row down the centre of a line of barn cloches. Remove the latter when the growth reaches the glass, by which time the risk of frost is past. At the end of May thin the early sorts to nine inches apart, the later ones to fifteen inches. When tillers or basal side shoots form, remove these, and there will be two cobs per stem, which in view of the spacing is a splendid yield. It is possible to get more cobs per plant by thinning to a wider spacing and allowing the tillers to develop. The yield per unit area of land, however, is usually not so heavy, as frequently the tillers are not good croppers.

VEGETABLE MARROWS RAISED UNDER CLOCHES. RECENTLY DE-CLOCHED

VEGETABLE MARROWS. The first cloche-raised marrows are ready to cut about the end of June from seed sown in the South in mid-April, at the end of the month in the Midlands, and in early May in the North. Space the seed two inches apart, and set it an inch deep under a barn cloche. When the seedlings have formed two or three normal leaves, transplant them to stations at three feet apart, prepared as advised for ridge cucumbers. Remove the growing points above the fifth leaf to induce side shoots, and thereafter nip out the growing points of straggling shoots. Take off the cloches when more room must be given, and at all times water copiously. It is helpful to pollinate the female flowers, especially in those districts in which bees are not numerous.

CELERY.   Celery seedlings for planting out in trenches may be raised in precisely the manner advised for celeriac. The white variety White Plume should be sown in the South in mid-February, in the Midlands at the end of the month, and in the North in mid-March. Follow with the variety Clayworth Prize a month later.

LEEKS.   Leeks may be raised for planting out in the same way as advised for onions. Sow the first batch in the South and Midlands in mid-January, in the North in early February, in all districts at the end of February and mid-March. Musselburgh is a first-rate early sort, while The Lyon is unequalled for late.

SPINACH.   Prickly spinach is the best for cloche work. It may be sown in the South in mid-January, in the Midlands in early February, and in the North in early March. Make the drills an inch deep and eight inches apart, using low barn cloches. Thin the seedlings to six inches apart, and if there is a dry Spring water well, or some of the plants will run to seed.

In mid-April sow New Zealand spinach in the Midlands and South, and in early May in the North. Set one row down the middle of barn cloches, making the drill an inch deep. Later thin the seedlings to two feet apart, and move the cloches when this much-spreading crop indicates that it must have more room.

PARSLEY.   A valuable herb that will be ready for picking in May if seed is sown in the South at the beginning of March, in the middle of the month in the Midlands, and at the end in the North. Use large tent cloches, and sow very thinly in a half-inch deep drill down the centre. Thin the seedlings gradually to a foot apart. Moss Curled is a good choice of variety. Sow again at the end of July under similar conditions for a Winter supply, selecting the well-known sort Myatt's Garnishing.

STRAWED STRAWBERRIES UNDER CLOCHES

CLOCHE CROP COMBINATIONS

Space under cloches is so valuable that not an inch of it should be wasted. Here are examples of the combinations that can be worked out. Sow or plant a row of lettuce or radishes along each side of broad, French, runner and haricot bean rows, sweet corn rows, and grow radishes on the ridge of newly planted potatoes. Shorthorn carrots may be sown amongst cloche-covered cauliflowers and cabbages, while turnips do remarkably well sown among newly planted vegetable marrows and ridge cucumbers.

INTERESTING NEW METHOD OF GROWING RASPBERRIES UNDER CLOCHES

The canes, three feet to four feet long and three feet apart in the rows, are tied down to each other. The rows were covered with Barn " F " size Chase Continuous Cloches at the end of January. The photograph, showing the Raspberries in bud was taken on the 11th March

A very attractive triple scheme is to broadcast shorthorn carrots very thinly under barn cloches. Plant a row of cauliflowers eighteen inches apart down the centre, and between and around the cauliflowers, lettuce seedlings at eight inches apart. The lettuce is soon ready, and after it is removed the cauliflowers and carrots do not compete with each other.

FRUIT CROPS

STRAWBERRIES. The plants should be covered with barn cloches in January, and fruit will be ripe on them six weeks before the outdoor fruit matures. As soon as the flowers have fallen, spread straw amongst the plants, and in dry weather water copiously. Generally speaking, no air is required until early May, but after that date open out the cloches a little. If the sun is very bright shade the glass slightly with whitewash, and gather the fruit as soon as it becomes ripe. Royal Sovereign is the most suitable sort.

RASPBERRIES. To obtain early raspberries stretch a wire twelve inches above ground level, and tie the canes to it. Take off six inches from the top of each. The canes can cross a little, but most not be overcrowded. It is highly important to water copiously when the fruits are swelling, and in this case, as in that of strawberries, the glass should be lightly shaded. Tall barn cloches are the most suitable, and there is no better variety than Lloyd George.